THE MOTIVATION CRISIS

Winding Down and Turning Off

JOHN R. HINRICHS

A DIVISION OF AMERICAN MANAGEMENT ASSOCIATIONS

Library of Congress Cataloging in Publication Data

Hinrichs, John R
  The motivation crisis; winding down and turning off.

  Includes bibliographical references.
  1. Job satisfaction.   2. Motivation (Psychology)
3. Personnel management.   I. Title.
HF5549.5.J63H5   658.31'4   73-90418
ISBN 0-8144-5357-0

First printing

PREFACE

SEVERAL YEARS AGO, a few colleagues and I at IBM met informally for a number of months to share some insights evolving from various personnel research studies, to relate these to work being done in other organizations and universities, and to distill implications from these experiences for the future operations of large industrial organizations. Our discussion was far-ranging, much of it was "blue sky," little of it ended in anything tangible, but most of it was thought-provoking and stimulating.

To some extent, this book flows out of those discussions. When the hue and cry about the blue collar blues, the white collar woes, and the executive blahs began to recur in the press in the early 1970s, when Senator Kennedy focused the attention of a Congressional Subcommittee on Worker Alienation on the noneconomic needs of the workforce, and when job enrichment became the newest darling of the behavioral sciences, those discussions began to seem less and less blue sky. So the book evolved as a result of the rethinking about employee motivation.

Although there is controversy over the extent or even existence of the motivation crisis, and some contention that all we need in the United States is a good, hard recession to get people fully committed to their jobs, my experience and rather extensive familiarity with research on employee motivation and job satisfaction in U.S. and European industry convinces me that the problem is real. And it will not evaporate in a recession, as many members of industrial society seem to hope.

Most industries today, in the United States and abroad, are in a productivity crunch. Costs keep going up and competition keeps getting stronger. The phenomenal productivity growth of U.S. industry over the past hundred years has been largely through technological improvements and managerial efficiency. However, the incremental productivity through labor-saving devices that we have parlayed so effectively in the past gets harder and harder to find. There still is plenty of room for productivity gains through automation—especially in office environments—but nothing like the giant step Henry Ford made when he introduced the auto assembly line. In addition, in the 1970s it appears that we may be just about at the limit in terms of employee acceptance of new, sweeping efforts at efficiency through job redesign. It may seem efficient to design work so that employees perform clearly delineated, simple tasks, technology flow paces the expenditure of worker effort, and people, in effect, are extensions of machines. But today, such jobs are more and more seen as dehumanizing, oppressive, and trivial.

The new view of work is emerging as part and parcel of the rapidly changing social scene—a workforce swelled with more and more young, highly educated workers, unprecedented affluence and security, and the attitude that meaningful work is a birthright, rather widespread distrust of authority, incredible personal mobility, instant communications, and social values that more and more say that the quality of life is what makes life worth living. In the new social scene, the quality of work is increasingly being bound up in the total concern over the quality of life. It is a real issue.

In this book, I have tried to outline in more detail why the quality of work is of such concern and what the major dimensions of the issue are. I have also attempted to review three major strategies that may be used to address the issue. The interlocking perspectives of individual development, job development, and organization development can carry an organization quite far in its efforts to counter the declining commitment to work. In the last chapter, I have tried to highlight some of the blue-sky discussions my colleagues and I engaged in several years ago. I hope I haven't done violence to their ideas.

Special thanks are due my secretaries in Holland who prepared the manuscript: Saskia Ijpeij and Lilianne Dooijes. And of course thanks to my colleagues: William Alper, Richard Dunnington, William Penzer, David Sirota, and Alan Wolfson.

John R. Hinrichs

For Peggy

CONTENTS

INTRODUCTION

THE ONLY CONSTANT in our society is change. Change is one of the most pervasive themes we hear about today—it has become very *au courant* to point out how the moral values that have shored up our society are coming unglued, how technology is expanding geometrically, how "senior citizens" (anyone over 30) are ossified to the point where they are hopelessly out of touch with youth, how instant communications, jet travel, and multinational business are shrinking the world. Such concepts of change form the core of both popular and scholarly publications that appear on the best-seller lists for a surprising length of time: *Future Shock; The Year 2000; The Greening of America; The Limits to Growth*, to name a few.

The growing interest in change crops up in the concepts, concerns, and catchwords of intellectuals. Educators talk about the "half-life of engineers," sociologists talk about "galloping variables," and theologians talk about the "death of God." And the average citizen sees and feels change all about him—the flow of events reported daily, the flood of technological advances, the push and pull of politics in the nation and the world, and the new strains and concerns of parents trying to maintain stability and direction in dealing with their children. There can be little doubt that the world is in a process of rapid change.

Not long ago, most people reacted to change with passive acceptance; although they expressed concern over the disruption of comfortable, established life patterns, they tended to feel that many of the changes were inevitable.

Now a different reaction to the change process is emerging. Although people still accept the inevitability of many changes, they are trying to understand the underlying forces at work. Instead of merely adapting to those forces, they are determined to channel them in positive directions.

The field of futurism is one of the most striking new approaches in recent years to result from this new attitude toward change. Futurism is a dramatic, rapidly growing attempt to identify the forces for change in our society, their interactions, and their probable future courses. Equipped with this knowledge, people of action are trying to apply leverage to insure that changes move in desired directions.

Futurism started in U.S. government "think tanks" such as the Rand Corporation. In these settings futurism focused mainly on military and political systems. In 1967 the publication of *The Year 2000* (Macmillan), by Herman Kahn and Anthony Wiener of the Hudson Institute, thrust the movement into the public limelight.

Now the futurist movement is well established on the

American scene as well as overseas. A number of Delphi techniques are under way to attempt to forecast the future. With this process the most knowledgeable people in a particular field of study are surveyed through iterative questionnaires to narrow down on what is believed to be the probable future course of events. The Institute for the Future at Middletown, Connecticut, specializes in this technique. The field has even matured to the point where it has its own journal, *The Futurist*.

Futurist activity is one of the most exciting new intellectual activities. But it is more than just an academic exercise.

Futurism recognizes that many of the problems in our society today stem from our past insufficient concern about the future. Unconstrained technology, urban sprawl, air and water pollution, and ecological imbalances are the result of our passively stumbling into the future instead of anticipating and controlling the direction of our evolution. Futurists are concerned with before-the-fact deterrents rather than with the reactive solutions we must employ today: consumerism and political lobbies, an energy "crisis," crash programs, and legislation dealing with air and water pollution. Morever, they recognize the universal nature of these problems. The air pollution that makes Tokyo almost uninhabitable and the ugly waters of the Rhine River are classic examples of indifference to the future.

Beyond just direct interest in the future is our growing recognition of the need to examine the interaction of the factors that affect our society and how they change together. This need is particularly evident in the concern with ecosystems, where factors that seemingly affect only one aspect of the ecology actually branch out into many areas. The futurist movement takes a multifaceted view of change and is involved in a broad assessment of underlying factors and their interactions.

The accelerating pace of change has also spurred the increased interest in futurism. It has become obvious that the time span for corrective action is decreasing and that the change process must be evaluated and where necessary diverted as soon as possible.

It has also become evident that the resources available to undertake corrective programs are finite. Change is taking place on so many fronts and in so many different ways that intervention in every area is impossible. More and more we recognize the need to maximize our influences by selecting intelligently the most crucial areas of concern.

Thus the field of futurism emphasizes a positive orientation whereby man is seen as attempting to control his destiny rather than being buffeted by the forces of change. The goals of futurism are to understand change, and to plan and act to make the future more livable.

Thus far, futurism has focused principally on factors affecting society at large, such as technology, social and political systems, and economics. Now, however, the movement is being felt in industrial and business organizations. It is being tied in with the concepts of management by objectives and organization planning. Implications for the ability of organizations to attract, retain, motivate, develop, and fully utilize their human resources in a period of change are being drawn from futurists' projections of the shape of our society in the years ahead.

This book takes a futurist viewpoint in drawing together traditional management concepts as they affect the utilization of manpower in today's organization and considers how they must be revised to meet the probable changes in tomorrow's organization. We shall discuss what appear to be the salient threads of change and where they can be seen to be heading over the next five to ten years. Most of these individual threads are clear-cut today. Taken together they form a dramatic picture of the extent of organizational flux and a sharp view of how different the world of tomorrow will be from the world of yesterday and today.

Chapter 2 documents what seems to be the current state of worker motivation to participate in the economic and productivity objectives of American industry. The conclusion is that an employee motivation crisis exists and that, clearly, it will get worse. The suggestion is that bold, sweeping, and broad organizational changes are needed, now, to reverse this trend.

The next chapter outlines a motivation system intended as a basis for understanding the critical variables that must be considered in combating the motivation crisis. We attempt to identify leverage points for management to use in influencing the motivation process in the organizations of today and tomorrow.

Chapter 4 deals with the very root of many motivation problems—the new employee's entry into the organization. It describes the specific kinds of work he is expected to perform and is especially concerned with young "knowledge workers."

The next three chapters deal with three specific

aspects of the present motivation crisis: the loss of both motivation and job satisfaction, attrition, and skills obsolescence. A model of the change process traces the steps that lead to these various outcomes.

Chapters 8 through 10 deal with three main approaches to overcoming the motivation crisis: personnel development, job development, and organization development. The concluding chapter sketches new models of organizations, showing the direction in which the system must evolve to adequately cope in the future. These models incorporate the three development programs discussed earlier, but the chapter reviews additional forms that may help an organization meet the demands of tomorrow.

THE
MOTIVATION
CRISIS

1

THE CHANGING INDUSTRIAL SCENE

IT IS APPROPRIATE to begin with a brief review of the major trends in the nature of the workforce and their implications for management today and tomorrow as seen by the futurists. Not all these trends are new, and few are startling by themselves. Taken together, they form a comprehensive picture of where we are today and where we seem to be going. This overview will not be a bold prediction of the future—that would be risky if not impossible—but an extrapolation of current trends to suggest how different the world already is from just a few years ago. From this comparison of yesterday and today, we should be able to draw a broad, very general outline of the future.

DEMOGRAPHY

Change in the basic structure of the American workforce is one of the most striking dimensions of change at present. Many changes have been taking place for a long time and many are well recognized: the movement of manpower out of agriculture, the increase in the percent of the labor force engaged in services, the growth of white collar workers, and the increasing numbers of blacks and women in the labor force. The growing number of young workers represents perhaps the most dramatic change.

AGE

Between 1970 and 1980, dramatic changes in the number of workers in each key age bracket in the workforce will take place. For example, while the total workforce is expected to increase by 17.3 percent during that ten-year period, young workers under age 35 will account for most of this increase (48.4 percent for those in the 25- to 34-year-old bracket and 30.7 percent for workers between ages 20 and 24, as opposed to 11.9 and 3.3 percent respectively for the two age groups 35 to 44 and 45 to 54).[1] These figures indicate a continuation of the trends that took place during the latter part of the 1960s. Thus we have seen large increases in the number of young people in the workforce; we will see more.

There are profound implications for the need for more effective motivational systems in organizations. With the premium on early identification of management potential over the last decade, young (between 25 and 34 years old) people have been promoted rapidly into executive positions. As a result, the middle and upper levels of many organizations are filled with fast-risers with 30 years or more of active business life ahead of them.

But where are they going to go over those next 30 years? The higher one rises, the fewer his opportunities for advancement. Moreover, the workers in this age bracket are also blocked by the relatively stable number of people between 35 and 44 holding key executive positions. Obviously, many of the young people in middle management positions just will not move up. And as they sit there, they will tend to stagnate, their motivation will wind down, they will become frustrated when their fast-starting careers seem to have run out of gas. But they will tend to hold onto what they have; they too will become "blockers" in the organizations. Those from the 20- to 24-year bracket will in turn find themselves bumping against a solid layer of entrenched incumbents. The result can only be frustration and stagnation on their part as well.

With the destruction of employee morale and aspirations, the organization will face severe consequences. Lack of mobility implies rigidity of the system. Creativity and innovation will gradually wither. New ideas and new blood will not find their way into the system unless the organization expands naturally with a general growth in the economy. But the economy is expected to grow only modestly, at least as far as manpower requirements are concerned. Providing new sources and forms of personal growth to prevent employee and organization stagnation is one of the greatest challenges facing the managers of tomorrow.

EDUCATION

Today, one out of every four Americans of college age is actively enrolled in college-level instruction. By 1980, 50 percent of this group probably will be enrolled. Emphasis on education represents a tremendous investment. "The total spent on higher education in the U.S. is up from $4.2

billion in 1956 to $28 billion in 1972. Fifteen years ago, U.S. colleges granted fewer than 300,000 Bachelor-level degrees and fewer than 10,000 doctorate degrees. This year [1972] those totals [have] climbed respectively to one million and 300,000 and that rate of growth is expected to continue for many years." [2]

Without doubt, this level of investment has contributed handsomely to the tremendous growth rate of the U.S. economy during the 1950s and 1960s. At the same time, higher education is no longer viewed as a privilege but as a right that must be extended to all those who want it. The question, however, is whether we can continue to get full return on this investment, whether we can provide enough meaningful jobs to meet the higher expectations that half of the nation's young people bring to the labor market.

With the recession in 1969 came the first hint of an overabundance of skills in the United States. Not since pre-World War II days had recruiters failed to clamor for applicants at college placement offices. College recruiting is picking up, but the indications are that it will not return to the level of the earlier 1960s. Recruiting now tends to be more selective and much less competitive than it was during the 1950s and 1960s.

The signs are that the problem will probably get worse. "A federal task force on higher education estimates that by 1977, every recognized profession will have an oversupply of new graduates. Even the perennial shortage of doctors will end by 1978, says the Health, Education, and Welfare Department." [3]

These trends suggest that increasingly young people

will enter the workforce with high expectations that are, in the face of reality, unwarranted. Already many young people have faced a rude shock after completing their education and beginning to look for work. When they finally have to settle for work below their expectations and levels of ability and training, the results can only be broadly based dissatisfaction and alienation. Most likely they will turn off from their work before even starting it. The effect will tend to be cumulative throughout the workforce. Even people without higher education will have raised aspirations that will be difficult to meet; with semiskilled jobs going to college graduates, there will be few opportunities for nongraduates to find attractive positions.

Overeducation and underutilization of skills indicate, very emphatically, the need to upgrade the jobs we offer. Just as we must find new forms and sources of personal growth, we must direct our attention toward finding new forms and sources of challenge in the work we ask people to do.

Technology

Most Americans recognize the important role technology has played in the growth of our economy, particularly in glamour projects such as the Apollo program, the tremendous increases in computer capability, and the growing applications of nuclear energy. Beyond these very visible technological achievements is the awareness of the vital contribution technology has made to our ability to compete in world markets.

The prominence of technology in our economy is best

illustrated by the increase in R&D expenditures in the United States since World War II, especially during the 1960s. For example, between 1960 and 1972 R&D expenditures doubled from $13.7 billion in 1960 to $29 billion in 1972. The rate of R&D expenditures flattened in the recession period 1969 to 1971 because of declines in federal technology programs and the general business downturn. In 1973 R&D expenditures picked up to an expected rate of $31 million, and the National Science Foundation estimates a 25 percent increase by 1975.[4]

Significantly, from the standpoint of manpower needs, most of the renewed emphasis on R&D is anticipated in selected project areas designed to achieve national goals. The era of big projects like Apollo and the SST are not expected to consume much of the new R&D expenditures. Instead, emphasis will be on projects like the creation of economical new energy sources, the development of a pollution-free car, the development of more viable transportation systems, recycling, the industrial application of atomic power, and the creation of gas from coal. Selected technological skills rather than increased manpower will be required.

The continued emphasis on technology will have major implications for the utilization of skills. First, the selective nature of R&D will cause increasing imbalances between the supply and demand of specific skills. More long-range manpower planning will be required. More flexibility will be needed in the restructuring or upgrading of skills. And less rigid bureaucratic structures and practices will be needed, with emphasis redirected to providing authority, recognition, and rewards based on competence.

Second, with technology changing constantly and the geometric progression of knowledge continuing, organizations that neglect the maintenance and upgrading of skills will find that their key manpower resource will rapidly become obsolete.

Thus we may expect new concern with the prevention of skills obsolescence, new thinking about an educational process that views training as a continuous process rather than merely the launching of a career, and new concepts of careers, with people more and more engaging in several fields of activity throughout a working life rather than settling into a single field.

THE ECONOMY

Several aspects of present trends and future expectations in the economy as a whole have strong implications for skills motivation and utilization in tomorrow's organization. First, it is generally conceded that the U.S. economy will grow, at least in the immediate future. Just as the downturn of 1969, 1970, and 1971 can be looked on as a "blip" on the overall growth trends, which began to level off with the economic pickup in 1972 and 1973, not even the jolt of a worldwide energy "crisis" and pervasive inflation alter the basic long-term prospects for substantial and sustained economic growth. There is basically broad optimism about growth and confidence in the future.

The growing affluence of Americans is another major

factor with implications for skills motivation. Between 1965 and 1980, there will have been a 50 percent increase in real terms in the median family income. At the same time, the great disparity between the haves and have-nots will grow wider. This trend, reflected on a worldwide scale, represents one of the most severe potential world problems for the decades ahead.

Because society becomes more complex every day, the manager must coordinate his role with a great many functions that affect what he does and how he does it. More viable methods and approaches for dealing with the many interfaces of government, law, R&D, marketing, and so forth need to be developed. The added dimension of increasing multinational business and the necessity for building interfaces between different cultures and societies indicate further need for coordinating and integrating functions.

In the face of these general economic trends, workers will approach their jobs, as well as life in general, with a lower tolerance for frustration. In an affluent society, people will be less inclined to passively accept poverty, unemployment, poor health care, and so on. A paycheck, a job—a decent job—for every American will be viewed as a right, not a privilege.

As a result of affluence and economic growth we may expect new sources of motivation and satisfaction. It is happening already, but the pace will accelerate. Adequate pay will be just an expected part of the working relationship; it will have little motivational effect. Only intrinsically challenging work will be capable of instilling motivation and providing job satisfaction.

Finally, new forms of authority will be needed to co-ordinate and integrate the complex sets of relationships within which organizations must function. There will be a need for continuing systematic attention to maintaining harmony among those relationships.

SOCIETAL TRENDS

Daniel Bell, a well-known sociologist, has succinctly outlined some of the key trends characterizing our society.[5]

1. The life of the *individual* today is *embedded in organizations*. In 1960, only one out of seven males in the United States was self-employed; 85 percent of the labor force worked for wages and salaries paid by others. Just two decades earlier, in 1940, one out of four males was self-employed. The trend is continuing in which people work in organizations in a framework of authority relationships, unable to determine and control all aspects of what they do.

2. Our society is one of *social density*. With 200 million persons in 1970 and continuing growth, many of the facilities and resources available are strained almost to the point of crisis: air and water pollution, overextended transportation facilities, and the energy crisis, not to mention filled-to-capacity campgrounds in our national parks or a postal system that just about grinds to a halt each Christmas.

3. We have become a *national society*, and increasingly an international society. Within the past 25 years, jet travel, national television, national government concern with things like health care, education, and welfare have

led to mobility unheard of just a few decades ago. With this mobility and the breaking down of the smaller community has come an increased sense of rootlessness.

4. We have also become a *communal society* rather than a melting pot. It has been recognized that the concept of homogeneity of all persons in the society just does not fit the facts. Increasingly, pressures from special-interest groups are brought to bear to achieve the interests of individuals. Individuals realize that by themselves they can have little influence on the course of events; by banding together, they find their influence magnified tremendously. While freedom for the individual is one of the things which people in our society are actively seeking, at the same time the facts of life force us to depend on group membership for exerting influence on a broader society.

5. We are well into the period of *post-industrial society*. In post-industrial society, the major part of the economy is engaged in services rather than the production of goods, the technical and professional class is expanding more rapidly than others, and innovation and policy making become dependent on theoretical knowledge. The emphasis is on human capital, and the knowledge worker is seen as the key to productivity. Post-industrial society is a further step in the evolution of our society, which has already evolved from an agricultural to an industrial orientation.

6. We are experiencing increasing *leisure* in our society. With more holidays, shorter workweeks, and an orientation toward using the affluence of our society, people have more time to concentrate on nonwork activities.

7. We are also a *learning* society. Education has always played a major role in our society, but it will play

more of a role in terms of adult education, preparation for career changes, and skills updating. The effects of continuing learning and growth will be felt in industry.

These general trends show that work, in its traditional form, is becoming less central to the lives of people, more and more of whom choose jobs with organizations rather than venture self-employment. With additional leisure and more concern with learning and personal growth, people will increasingly seek alternate means to self-fulfillment. At the same time the loss of identity created by social density and the trend toward a communal and a national society will lead people to seek individuality and stability wherever they can; they will demand more personal satisfaction from their work. Similarly, there will be increased emphasis on learning and development in the workplace. Organizations that fail to satisfy these needs will discover their valuable employees all too willing to change jobs.

Against this framework the challenge to organizations for building new forms of motivation into the working relationship is very real, perhaps urgent.

Changes in Values

The changes taking place in our society pose severe challenges to the existing order of things, particularly in business organizations. Again, Daniel Bell outlines a number of these challenges.[6]

1. *Challenge to authority.* This challenge was already very evident in the problems in the universities during the 1960s, protests against government defense policies and

practices, riots in the center cities, and the continuing crisis between minority group members and the police.

One of the primary causes of the growing challenge to authority is presumed "hypocrisy" on the part of many of the leaders of our society. The protesters have pointed to the war in Vietnam, price fixing in industry, corruption in government, political espionage, and the gap between civil rights law and fact, as examples.

The other source of the challenge to authority revolves around legitimacy, and the question of legitimacy will undoubtedly be behind the growing challenge in business. Formerly, management was legitimate because of ownership. Now the authority of management is being increasingly questioned, and authoritarian roles in business are less acceptable. Where coercive power used to be applied, more and more expert power is being demanded. There is a very clear possibility that this questioning of the legitimacy of authority in business will come to the forefront in a broader challenge to authority throughout our society. Whereas in the 1960s the action was in the universities and in the civil rights area, in the 1970s it may well move to business organizations.

2. *Challenge to traditional organization.* The traditional forms of hierarchy and bureaucracy are increasingly being seen as ineffective, dehumanizing and unresponsive to the needs of organization members. The old structures of division of labor, "line" versus "staff" organizations, formal chains of authority and of "reporting to" a particular manager are too clearly reminiscent of the military milieu from which they were borrowed decades ago. The concepts are increasingly rejected by younger people coming into orga-

nizations, not to mention by more senior employees who recognize the need for a more fluid, looser, task-oriented form of organization. In large measure, the growing anti-business sentiment in the United States reflects a rejection of the bureaucratic model, as well as a rather broad belief that American business is too profit-minded at the current time. The challenge to organization will force some changes to the traditional forms.

3. *Participation.* More and more people in organizations are demanding a voice in influencing their own roles and their futures. It is seen in the external community—in the churches, social agencies, school boards, poverty programs, and so forth. Demands for participation are growing in business. First, with the increasing education and competence of people in the workforce there is more recognition that people *do* have the ability to make appropriate decisions that affect their own work careers and roles. Second, findings of the behavioral sciences have for a number of years been emphasizing the positive aspects of participation in decision making. These concepts are increasingly being advanced at universities, in the management literature, and in management development courses. The demand for more participation is picking up.

To the extent that people do not feel they are able to influence their careers and their roles, they are turning off to organizations. Some of the most capable new graduates in the United States now are more oriented toward following a craft or going into one of the professions such as law or medicine than toward pursuing careers in business. A major reason, in addition to questioning the legitimacy of authority and the distaste for hierarchy and bureaucracy, is the extent to which they feel they would be unable to participate in important decisions affecting them within the business environment. More genuine participation will have to be built into organizations to attract these capable people.

4. There is a large amount of *anti-scientism* in the current social scene. There have always been mixed feelings toward science and technology in the United States; while we like very much the benefits of technology, there is a basic mistrust of "eggheads" and "intellectuals." To many people today, technology is seen as having gone too far. The negative effects of technology in the form of pollution or the unexpected consequences from use of DDT have suggested to some that technology is out of control and that it is overriding more humanistic values. This has been followed by some reactions against the expert. The ecology movement, consumerism, and concern for organizational responsibility in social issues are direct challenges to organizations and must be dealt with.

5. *Personalism*. This is another challenge to traditional structures. There is a reaction to the de-personality of the mobile society, the alienation and loneliness of people, and the drying up of affect and a belief that the society blocks the flowering of individual emotions and feelings. This challenge can be seen in a growing new humanism and a concern with sensitivity, openness, encounter, and trust. The concern with returning humanism to contemporary life is part of the system of values that will be felt more and more in organizations.

6. *Life-style*. In this country and in the world our life-style has become much freer than just a few years ago.

Not only is there a more liberal attitude toward sex; in general the increasing orientations toward hedonism, existentialism, and the "here and now" are challenging the traditional patterns of deferred gratification. Such values will also be felt in the demands people bring to organizations.

The implications of these changing value systems for organizations are profound. The old work ethic is being challenged. Other factors are seen as more important in one's life. Also, there is a direct questioning of our priorities. We are unwilling to permit technology a free rein. We no longer accept the overriding primacy of the profit motive. And we now recognize that some degree of planning and control is necessary to insure that industry and business serve broader national objectives rather than pure self-interest.

Similarly, the willingness to challenge traditional institutions is now well established. At no time in the past, except in the formal emerging union movement, has the willingness to protest been as evident as it is today.

The trends affecting the business environment present major challenges to traditional organizations. A young, highly educated, highly expectant workforce with low frustration tolerance, in an environment of high technology, complexity, rapid change, and high affluence, with low tolerance for unemployment and maldistribution of rewards, and a post-industrial society with an emphasis on learning, leisure, and mobility—all add up to extremely strong forces for change.

Some aspects of our society have adapted, or are in

the process of adapting. The universities, for example, have certainly changed over the past decade. Businesses, however, have not adapted very much. It is really surprising the extent to which the bureaucratic forms of current organizations have remained pretty much the same as they were 50 years ago. There has been some movement in the equal employment opportunity area, in the employment of women, in self-righteous pronouncements about participative management, in tentative experiments with concepts like matrix organizations. But in fact little has changed. If industrial and business organizations do not change voluntarily over the next decade, they probably will be forced to. The forces for change are pervasive and strong.

REFERENCES

1. U.S. Department of Labor, *Manpower Report of the President* (Washington: U.S. Government Printing Office, 1972).
2. "The Job Gap for College Graduates in the '70's," *Business Week*, September 23, 1972, pp. 48–58.
3. Ibid., p. 50.
4. "U.S. Know-how Is on the Move Once More," *U.S. News & World Report*, January 22, 1973.
5. Daniel Bell, "They're Talking About Our Future. Shall We Listen?" *Think*, February 1971.
6. Ibid.

2

TURNING OFF

For the past few years U.S. industry has been experiencing a severe motivation crisis, which is evident from the continuous stream of articles both in the general press and in professional and management journals. The recurrence of "boredom," "monotony," and "discontent" in the titles of those articles reflects the extent of the crisis.

At a time when wages and fringe benefits are at all-time highs, when sophisticated production processes have removed most of the onerous, heavy manual demands from industrial jobs, when our living standard is providing more comfort than we have ever had, and when we are moving into a period of increased leisure and four-day workweeks, more and more American workers at all levels are turning off to their jobs. Too often they find their jobs at best uninteresting, at worst a repetitive, grinding oppression.

The symptoms of the motivation crisis are quite tangible: increasingly shoddy output, high absenteeism (as much as 13 percent in some auto plants, against only 3 percent not too long ago), strikes, which more and more focus on noneconomic issues, and high turnover (as much as 30 percent in some white collar industries). The result is a drain on industry's financial profits and the loss of its ability to compete effectively in world markets.

Most of the attention to the problem focuses on the blue collar worker, especially the auto worker. No doubt the auto assembly line is far from an ideal work situation. Tasks have been specialized to the point of being trivial; jobs have been made repetitive, paced, and closely disciplined. In fact, jobs on the line embody all the dehumanizing aspects of modern industrial society.

Most people work on the line by necessity, not by choice, strictly for money and security. But generally those goals have been attained through the labor union battles of the 1930s and 1940s. Today other objectives are moving to the fore. Now that the security and earnings battle has been won, increasingly labor–management conflict in the auto industry will revolve around the work itself; the motivation crisis has filled the void.

Is Anybody Happy?

There are clear signs that the crisis has spread to other groups. White collar workers (file clerks, secretaries, typists, and so on) are becoming restless. A recent survey by the Opinion Research Corporation (ORC) covering 25,000 employees in 85 firms showed sharp declines in white collar job satisfaction since 1966.[1]

According to the ORC study, the largest declines in job satisfaction since 1966 were in employees' evaluations of their job security (14 percent more persons expressed concern) and ratings of pay (17 percent were more dissatisfied). The analysis also showed sharp drops in white collar workers' confidence in management's willingness to deal fairly with their problems or in the effectiveness of communications to or from management. The greatest declines were in confidence in the concern and responsiveness of top management, with immediate supervision being seen in roughly the same light as in 1966. In short, the study found, many white collar employees are increasingly beginning to feel like cogs in a great impersonal bureaucracy.

Traditionally, white collar employees have identified with management, and have expressed little interest in belonging to unions. The patterns of alienation shown in these survey' results, however, suggest an environment ripe for union organizing efforts. Trends for the 1960s suggest that dwindling motivation is finding expression in union activity. Between 1958 and 1968, for example, white collar union membership increased 46 percent to 3,179,000. Whether the 1970s and 1980s will be an era of strong white collar unionization remains to be seen, but certainly such pervasive dissatisfaction will have a powerful impact on many aspects of business operations. No longer can management afford to take for granted the commitment and dedication of its white collar workforce.

Similarly, dissatisfaction among many professional workers is on the upsurge. Not too many years ago, strikes, or job actions, by school teachers or welfare workers were unheard of. Now they are commonplace.

The well-documented job discontent of engineers and

technical employees found expression in high turnover and professional unionism—at least until the job market crunch in 1969 and 1970.[2] But there is no reason to believe that the problems have disappeared with the decline of turnover. In the 1970s many engineers undoubtedly continue to feel that their careers are stagnant and that their jobs are routine, requiring little creativity and underutilizing their skills and training.

Job dissatisfaction is widespread even among highly educated scientists and research people. In a recent study 20 percent of a nationally representative group of Ph.D.'s in industrial chemical research just eight years out of graduate school reported overall dissatisfaction with their jobs; 9 percent expressed indifference.[3] Only 8 percent of a comparable group of new Ph.D.'s who went into academic jobs reported negative attitudes.

Two other research projects concluded that the winding down process pervades all levels of American business. One study was carried out at the University of Michigan Institute for Social Research using data from over 1,000 nationally representative interviews. Comprehensive analysis of the data, originally collected for the U.S. Department of Labor as a survey of working conditions, revealed: "Vulnerability to blue collar blues is endemic to the whole workforce and rests only slightly on the stereotyped attributes of the middle-mass worker."[4]

The second study, conducted by the W. E. Upjohn Institute for Employment Research under a grant from the Department of Health, Education, and Welfare, also found pervasive job dissatisfaction at all levels of the U.S. workforce. The study concluded that an outright majority of Americans—including white collar workers and even middle-level executives—are profoundly dissatisfied with their jobs.[5]

OTHER CAUSES OF DISCONTENT

Possibly some widespread job dissatisfaction is a spinoff of general dissatisfaction with a variety of components of contemporary life. For example, a nationwide sample conducted by the Gallup Poll Organization showed that job satisfaction had declined by 6 percent, on the average, between 1969 and 1971.[6] The decline was 13 percent for black Americans. There were also clear indications of lower job satisfaction among young, low-income city people. In this sample, declining satisfaction with the job accompanied declining satisfaction with income and housing.

EVEN EXECUTIVES GO AWOL

A *Newsweek* article shows that the motivation crisis has reached the executive suites of some of our larger organizations.[7] Apparently because of job alienation and the need to withdraw from the pressures of organization life, more and more executives go AWOL from time to time, using a number of ruses to get out of the office to attend movies, play golf, or shop during work hours.

The most tangible indicator of dissatisfaction in managerial and executive ranks has been reflected in thriving executive placement activity and high turnover, at least during the dynamic decade of the 1960s. The early 1970s, however, finds the executive job market significantly depressed; indications are that it probably will not regain the fluidity of the 1960s. If this is true, executives will have less opportunity to relieve their job frustration and sustain their motivation through rapid internal promotion or the recourse of moving elsewhere if necessary. The very clear probability of continued depressed mobility potential for middle managers may be as critical an aspect of the motivation crisis now and through the rest of the 1970s as the much publicized blue collar blues or dissatisfaction among white collar workers and engineers. Declining managerial motivation strikes at the core of the structure that makes American business go, the cadre who can translate executive policy decisions and plans into tangible results.

Three key factors are at work in the evolving managerial motivation crisis. First, there was a dearth of management talent during the 1960s, primarily because the low birth rate during the depression resulted in a shortage of potential executives in the age bracket 30 to 40. Thus in the past decade the pool of candidates for each available middle management position was small. Competition was mild, and managers became accustomed to rapid advancement either within their own companies or in other organizations. As a result of this high mobility, many key jobs today are held by young executives with a long time to go before retirement.

Second, during the 1970s the bulge of potential executives born in the 1940s (the baby boom era) will be vying for whatever openings occur. The much larger pool of candidates will mean more competition and less rapid movement.

Third, managerial openings result from general economic growth. During the 1970s many programs and projects requiring extensive executive talent—civil and military aerospace programs, the Apollo project, burgeoning educational facilities, and so on—have been phased out or cut back. In all likelihood, the new top priority projects for this decade will require greater inputs of blue collar talent rather than managerial talent—pollution control, development of energy sources, updating of utilities, and the like. Major emphasis probably will be on mature industries where growth will require only limited additional managerial talent. The increasing automation of many middle managerial roles and activities will also reduce manpower demands.

So in the face of an increasing supply of and probably a stable or decreasing demand for middle managers, coupled with goals and norms of rapid advancement carried over from the 1960s, the makings of a severe morale and motivation crisis among managers are with us now. The implications for business are profound. If managerial commitment begins to wind down, accompanied by the broadscale turning off of blue collar and white collar employees, what will happen to U.S. industry?

THE MOTIVATION CRISIS FOR YOUNG WORKERS

Industrial attitude surveys consistently find that new hires have relatively high job satisfaction shortly after joining their organization but that their motivation declines rather sharply within the first few years. If they remain with the company, in time there may be some reversal of those declines. The trends shown in Figure 1 are typical of the results obtained from industrial attitude surveys. Why do new employees' initial high levels of job satisfaction tend to decline in such a short time?

One explanation is that a psychological phenomenon probably is at work, according to a study of attitude change among new M.B.A. graduates of the Carnegie-Mellon University School of Industrial Administration.[8] This study is important; it illustrates some of the critical dynamics affecting satisfaction and motivation during an employee's first few years on the job. During the study each graduate was asked to evaluate the relative attractiveness of specific companies and to select the organization he believed would offer the greatest opportunity for him to attain his personal goals through a managerial job. Ratings were obtained at several points in time: while the student was still at the university, before his actual deci-

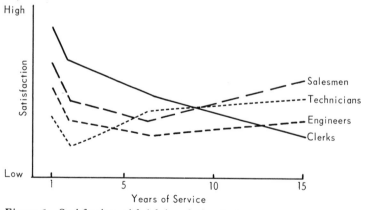

Figure 1. Satisfaction with job in relation to tenure.

sion to join a particular company; before he started work, but after his decision to accept the offer; one year after starting work; and three and a half years after starting work. A comparative analysis of the results of the four evaluation periods suggests some of the dynamics of attitude change among new managerial hires.

The first and second evaluations (before and after choosing a company, but before actually starting work) showed a significant increase in the graduates' ratings of attractiveness of the organization chosen and a downgrading of the organization rejected. The explanation is based on the theory of cognitive dissonance. The theory contends that when an individual must choose between two or more attractive alternatives, the process of choice creates dissonance. That is, an inconsistency is created in the person's mind by his awareness of the positive aspects of the alternative he did *not* choose and the negative aspects of the alternative he *did* choose. Such inconsistency is psychologically uncomfortable. To deal with it, the individual reevaluates the attractiveness of the alternatives. The one he chose increases in attractiveness, while the alternative he rejected is downgraded. The process, experienced unconsciously, helps relieve the psychological discomfort of cognitive dissonance.

The cognitive dissonance hypothesis nicely explains the observed increases in the graduates' initial evaluations after they had made their choices.

When the Carnegie-Mellon graduates were surveyed one year later, however, on the average they evaluated their organizations much less favorably than either before or just after starting work. Surveyed again two and a half years later, they showed no recovery from depressed levels registered at year 1.

The results suggest rather abrupt (within just one year) and significant disillusionment with the organization chosen. Presumably running up against the facts of organization life would build a more realistic set of expectations. Quite the contrary: the trends are clearly negative and reflect the quick onset of a winding down process.

Particularly noteworthy, a third of the Carnegie-Mellon graduates had changed companies within the three-and-a-half-year period (none had changed when the one-year follow-up was made). Those who had changed jobs were significantly *more* satisfied with their new organizations than those who had not changed. Either their disillusioning initial experiences had taught them to make more selective choices or, more likely, they were again undergoing postdecision dissonance reduction.

At the three-and-a-half-year point, there were significant declines from levels of satisfaction at the one-year point on two key aspects: the graduates' evaluation of the organization's potential for providing advancement opportunities and high salary. Interestingly, the actual salary levels of these M.B.A.'s at the three-and-a-half-year point were not related to their satisfaction with their companies: the main issue seemed to be an apparent lack of opportunities.

Between the one-year and the three-and-a-half-year point the M.B.A.'s rated their companies much higher in terms of freedom from pressures to conform, freedom from close supervision, and feeling like part of a team.

34

These views seem to reflect a growing independence and the extent to which the individuals were able to shape their own work roles after some experience in their companies. However, the elements that failed to meet expectations—salary and advancement—tended to be evaluated as highly important goals, while the positive aspects that became more readily attainable—such as independence—were rated relatively low in importance.

So, the study shows, the dissonance process probably helps build unrealistically high expectations on the part of the employee as he enters the organization. Such lack of reality is helped along by special treatment and hard sell during the recruiting process, as well as by students' general lack of organizational experience as a base for developing a more realistic assessment of alternatives. As a result, the new employee comes to the job with his head in the clouds. Too often, as the general attitude trends reflect, he is in for a shock, and the winding down process starts.

Winding down has to lead somewhere. Experience and research suggest two major outcomes: (1) withdrawal from the scene or attrition (the employee changes jobs, becomes an AWOL manager, has excessive absence, and so forth) or (2) loss of motivation—the employee fails to exert effort and becomes obsolescent and ineffective. In effect, he "attrits" in place.

In the next few chapters we shall discuss some factors surrounding each of these unfortunate consequences. Throughout the discussion, we must bear in mind that the process is not inevitable. Management can prevent the winding down phenomenon. A number of approaches are examined in Chapter 4, where we deal with the employee's entry into the business world. Other possible management actions will be discussed in later chapters. First, let us look at some general aspects of motivation to establish a framework for understanding and coping with the specific aspects of the very real motivation crisis in American business.

REFERENCES

1. Opinion Research Corporation report to management, "Employee Relations: Signs of Increasing Discontent Among White Collar Workers," Princeton, N.J., May 1970.
2. For example: R. R. Ritti, *The Engineer in the Industrial Corporation* (New York: Columbia University Press, 1971).
3. J. R. Hinrichs, "Value Adaptation of New Ph.D.'s to Academic and Industrial Environments—A Comparative Longitudinal Study," *Personnel Psychology*, Autumn 1972, pp. 545–565.
4. Stanley E. Seashore and J. Thad Barnowe, "Collar Color Doesn't Count," *Psychology Today*, August 1972, p. 80.
5. "The Worker's Woes," *Newsweek*, January 1, 1973; H. L. Sheppard and N. Q. Herrick, *Where Have All the Robots Gone? Worker Dissatisfaction in the '70s* (New York: The Free Press, 1972).
6. The Gallup Poll, "Social Indicators Show Downtrend—Whites and Blacks Less Content with Lives than Two Years Ago," Princeton, N.J., September 26, 1971.
7. "The Absentee Executive," *Newsweek*, November 17, 1969.
8. V. H. Vroom and E. L. Deci, "The Stability of Post-Decision Dissonance: A Follow-up Study of the Attitudes of Business School Graduates," *Organizational Behavior and Human Performance*, January 1971, pp. 36–49.

3

WHAT IS MOTIVATION?

PROBABLY FEW AREAS of concern to modern managers have received as much attention as motivation. In one way or another, the subject pops up in reviews of the economics of productivity, in discussions of industrial relations and collective bargaining, in descriptions of compensation and incentive schemes, in discussions of marketing strategies and effectiveness, not to mention in the research findings of industrial and organizational psychologists. Everyone recognizes motivation as the glue that holds an organization together; it is the stuff of progress. And it certainly will remain a key component in the continued success of business organizations through the 1970s and into the 1980s.

Perhaps because so many people concerned with industrial management see motivation as a critical element the literature tends to be a mishmash. Each of the various functions or disciplines has a different ax to grind and, understandably, a different perspective. The economist tends to be concerned with motivation from the viewpoint of productivity—whatever contributes to output per manpower unit. The industrial relations specialist tends to look at the motivation to join—to affiliate either with the management of the enterprise or with a trade union. The marketing specialist is concerned with the hustle to find sales prospects, develop proposals, close the order. The compensation specialist is concerned with the reward aspect of motivation—at least the limited aspect of rewards in the form of pay and financial bonuses. And the industrial psychologist tends to focus on the basic needs and expectations of the members of the enterprise and the extent to which those needs are being satisfied by the particular organizational circumstances under consideration.

With so many viewpoints, it is small wonder that concepts of goals, drives, needs, rewards, expectancies, satisfactions, effort, productivity, and so forth float through the management literature relatively divorced from one another. It is as though individually they will provide some understanding of the concept of motivation, as though we expect the pieces of the puzzle to explain the total picture before we fit them together.

With a concept as important as motivation, perhaps it is natural to be impatient to use whichever piece of the puzzle seems to help clarify our particular area of concern. To link several pieces tends to complicate things. If understanding job satisfaction gives us some insight into why people work, then we should use it. We know that money is an important reward, so shouldn't we build comprehensive compensation systems on that fact?

Of course we should. But shouldn't we also learn how the pieces of the puzzle tie together? Isn't it possible that if we are able to specify the interrelationships among the subparts of the motivation process, we will be able to identify leverage points where managers can make things happen more predictably? Conversely, shouldn't it be possible to identify points where managers or organizations cannot make things happen, and reconcile ourselves to the fact that these are just not legitimate areas of management concern? And, especially important, don't we need some understanding of motivational concepts to adequately develop our vital managerial resources for the future?

In this chapter, we shall try to build a comprehensive model of the motivation process. Our intention will be to do so in as straightforward and simple a manner as possible. We shall avoid the jargon of the psychologist, and hope that in the process we do not violate any basic concepts. Finally, we shall attempt to show what this model means to the individual manager as he attempts to increase the level of motivation in his organization and direct it toward tomorrow's requirements. In the remainder of the book, we shall draw on this model in our discussion of specific factors important for the effective leadership and development of the young persons who will be the leaders of tomorrow's organizations.

Choice: The Outcome of Motivation

When we consider motivation, what we really are interested in is the process by which choices between alternatives are made. For it is when people make choices that things happen. Whether the results of such choices enhance or detract from the broader objectives of an organization is determined by the nature of the motivation behind those choices.

In looking at the choice process in business settings, we usually think of the conscious, rational weighing of alternatives. Certainly the classic executive role is built almost exclusively around this concept. The ideal model of the effective executive role is one of a rational decision-making process. In addition the model suggests that the effectiveness of executive choice is determined largely by the motivation of the decision maker and takes for granted some basic level of ability to insure the "right" decision.

But this model is inadequate for explaining the whole decision-making process. Nor can it by itself help us fully understand the dynamics of motivation. Unconscious factors also affect choice. Without recognizing them we cannot understand the motivation process. A man's personal needs, sometimes almost imperceptibly, often below his level of consciousness, influence his choice among several competing goals.

THREE KEY OUTCOMES

Three key outcomes are of concern to us in evaluating choice behaviors in organizations: quantity of work, or productivity; quality of work; and the satisfaction, or morale, derived from the job. All three outcomes play a vital role in business enterprises.

Employee actions to provide individuality in the work setting are familiar outcomes of, or choices resulting from, motivation: the choice to be productive, to do a good job, or to contribute to the goals of the enterprise, as opposed to the choice to coast, to withdraw, or to deliberately sabotage the productive capability of the organization. For example, production line employees in large measure choose to have high productivity or to restrict output, to come to work or to call in sick, or (an increasingly critical choice today) to produce high quality work or to turn out shoddy workmanship. Or there may be a direct choice to build excitement into production line jobs, where little exists naturally: to install an occasional red fender on a white automobile, to cross up the wiring on a control panel so strange things happen at the test station, or to insert an unanticipated branch and a personal message in some remote corner of a complex computer program. (Many computer programming jobs today are essentially production line operations, where employees are subject to much of the motivational malaise of auto workers.)

The other key choice we must consider in any review of motivation is the choice to join an organization or to leave it. Here we are concerned with why people come to work for a particular company and why they stay with or leave an organization. The motivational underpinnings of these choices are the satisfactions associated with the employment relationship. To understand the dynamics of these choices, we have to examine the concepts of morale and job satisfaction.

Why Care about Employee Morale?

A hard-nosed businessman might question the importance of morale—"If I get quality and quantity, why should I care how my people feel about their jobs?" This view is shortsighted for a number of reasons. First, of course, high employee morale enhances an organization's ability to maintain its workforce. Moreover, a highly committed workforce provides management with great flexibility to change the structure, practices, and objectives of the organization with relative ease, with the confidence that employees will support the changes. Also, an organization with highly committed employees probably has less industrial relations conflict and the concomitant time lost on strikes, effort devoted to handling formal grievances, and protracted negotiations. Besides those very practical business reasons, high morale and job satisfaction are intrinsically desirable, something an organization should strive to attain along with work quantity and quality.

In discussing the three important outcomes necessary to a healthy organization, we have already touched on some of their underlying motivational attributes. Our problem now is to tie together the concepts of needs, goals, rewards, and so on into a coherent system and then to explore this system to enhance organizational effectiveness.

The Basis of Behavior

Three levels of motivational factors affect the desired outcomes with which we are concerned:

1. *Needs, or drives,* the forces inside the individual that determine his behavior.
2. *Goals,* the tangible aspects of the real world toward which behavior is directed; to some extent these goals are under an individual's control.

3. *Rewards*, the motivational attributes directly under the control of the organization.

NEEDS, OR DRIVES

Needs stir up and energize people. They are the force that results in effort; clearly, without effort there can be no productivity. Needs may be conscious or unconscious, and are relatively beyond the direct control of the individual.

Theories about human needs contend, with some validation from research, that all human behavior is stimulated by unsatisfied needs. Other theories argue that some degree of unsatisfied need is always present in the typical human being, that the needs that stir us into activity operate logically, and that only a few basic needs underlie all behavior.

Abraham Maslow's well-known theory contends that the basic human needs fall into a hierarchy of importance. The lowest level of unsatisfied needs predominate in determining behavior; as the lower-level needs are effectively satisfied, they no longer serve as strong motivators and higher-level needs move into prominence.

Maslow's theory suggests that the most fundamental needs of all organisms are *physiological*—the need for food, drink, and so on; when they are unsatisfied they are the primary needs to which the organism attends. *Safety* needs are the next level in the hierarchy—the need for physical and psychological security. The theory holds that these predominate once the physiological needs have been largely attended to. The next level, *belonging*, or social needs, usually does not play a significant role in determining behavior until lower-order needs have been met. Above the belonging needs are *esteem* needs—the need for self-esteem and for esteem in the eyes of others. The highest need in the hierarchy is the need for *self-actualization*, for realizing one's own potential.

The theory contends that all these needs can be satisfied except the highest level, the need for self-actualization. In effect, the theory maintains, once an individual has conquered one challenge, climbed one mountain, attained one highly gratifying objective, his need for self-actualization is not satisfied; rather, other horizons open. Thus the motivating needs of typical human beings are never completely satiated; to a greater or lesser degree we are always stirred up, agitated, inclined to activity by some degree of unsatisfied needs. The potential for the desired behavior, behavior that contributes to corporate objectives of high commitment and work quantity and quality, is always there.

Another theory postulates that the need for achievement is the need most critical to organizational effectiveness.[1] According to this theory other important needs are the need for power and the need for affiliation.

The specific theory to which one subscribes is not particularly relevant. The only significant point is that there are forces within the individual that shape his behavior and result in effort designed to satisfy his needs. When motivation is viewed in this framework, it should be clear that motivation is not something an organization does to an individual. Managers do not motivate people. Motivation is something an individual brings to an organization.

The only influence organizations can have on motivation is in shaping goals and rewards. Goals determine the probability that an employee will focus his behavior in certain directions to satisfy his needs. Thus goals are one leverage point at which the motivational system can be influenced. Similarly, rewards are tangible elements of the environment that satisfy salient needs. Our overall model of motivation must in some way incorporate the concepts of goals and rewards as well as the concept of needs.

GOALS

Generally, behavior is directed toward goals—tangible things individuals perceive as tending to satisfy the needs that are stirring them up and energizing them. Consciously or unconsciously, all of us are trying to achieve certain goals that mesh with our basic underlying needs.

Considerable behavioral science research has demonstrated that employees are able to articulate the factors that are important to them and that serve as personal goals in their job activities. As might be expected, the goals that are most important to an individual depend largely on the needs operating most strongly at a particular time. Perhaps that explains the consistent and meaningful differences in the goals of various types of employees. For example, professionals in R&D laboratories tend to place greatest importance on job challenge and skills utilization; blue collar employees in manufacturing settings tend to be highly oriented toward goals that mesh with security needs.[2]

In most organizations today, the basic physiological needs have been met and are of relatively little concern to us. However, goals that resonate with all the other needs in Maslow's hierarchy have been found to be of greater or lesser importance in employee motivation.

Clearly, safety needs are reflected in employee behavior directed toward job security. Initially these needs were responsible for much union organizing activity and labor–management conflict (though certainly other needs also have played significant roles in labor relations issues). Unmet security needs influence behavior at all levels of today's organization. The manager who filters upward communications because he is afraid to give bad news to his superiors, the research director who is reluctant to authorize a new project because it may fail, the administrator who hesitates to question procedures lest he be seen as "difficult," and the first-line supervisor who blocks meaningful employee participation in decision making for fear of losing control—all may be reacting to the pressures of unmet security needs. The objective of such behavior is to insure their personal safety and well-being—either physical or psychological. Most often behavior resulting from unmet security needs detracts from rather than contributes to organizational objectives.

Certainly belonging, or social, needs are reflected in many of the goals people strive to fulfill in organizations. To mesh with these needs, today's organizations try to foster harmonious interpersonal relations. Fair and equitable treatment by management is a cornerstone of enlightened employee relations. Soundly conceived company policies and procedures and decent working conditions can give employees a sense of personal comfort and belonging.

In the modern industrial world, most people's safety and belonging needs are in large measure satisfied. Rather than serving as conscious goals toward which behavior is directed, equitable employee relations policies, decent working conditions, reasonably harmonious interpersonal relations, enlightened supervision, and a fair degree of job security are looked on essentially as birthrights. When an organization no longer provides these, today's mobile employees, especially managers and professionals, will tend to look elsewhere to attain their career objectives.

Goals that mesh with the higher needs, needs for esteem and for self-actualization, provide today's organization with its greatest motivational leverage. Such goals as inherently interesting and challenging work, an opportunity for personal growth and learning, a sense of personal achievement, the recognition of accomplishment, a degree of autonomy, and a chance for advancement are organizational attributes that tie directly to esteem and self-actualization needs. They are the factors an organization must deliberately build directly into its reward system if it intends to foster high levels of motivation and effective outcomes.

Because these factors are critically important, most of the remaining chapters focus on strategies for enhancing these attributes in today's organizations so that they will serve as viable goals for the members of tomorrow's organizations.

REWARDS

While goals are the attributes of the tangible world that employees strive toward to satisfy their needs, rewards may be thought of as the attributes of the tangible world that an organization makes available to employees. When the rewards an organization provides are identical with the goals employees seek, there is a perfectly functioning motivation system. When goals and rewards are incongruent, there is something less than full motivation.

Ideally, in shaping a motivation system an organization should provide rewards that encompass all the attributes discussed in our review of goals. Rather than thinking narrowly of pay or fringe benefits as the only rewards under its direct control, the company with highly motivated employees maximizes the reward value of harmonious interpersonal relations, formal and informal recognition to enhance esteem, job challenge, responsibility, training, job autonomy, promotion, and so forth. Such a company recognizes that anything less than this full spectrum of rewards will result in less than full motivation.

Traditionally, organizations have taken a relatively limited view of the nature of rewards. Managers have focused almost exclusively on pay. Recently, however, more and more managers have begun to consider the value of intangible rewards such as challenging work or job autonomy and to support programs designed to enhance those factors. In the years to come we may expect a great deal more of this reorientation.

THE MOTIVATION PROCESS

The motivational factors discussed so far—needs, goals, and rewards—are static. They describe some motivational attributes, but in themselves do not translate directly into the outputs with which we are concerned: work quantity, work quality, and morale. We have to identify the intervening processes by which these factors are translated into performance. Then we should examine some of the factors that filter these links either to the enhancement or detriment of the total motivation system.

Figure 2 shows how various components of the motivation process interact. The major links are (a) effort, or energy expenditure, (b) directed effort, or effective performance, and (c) satisfaction, or job and company commitment.

EFFORT

Effort indicates how hard people work, how much energy they expend toward attaining a particular goal. Effort is, of course, a prerequisite to high levels of productivity—our outcome objective of work quantity.

In general, effort reflects the strength of the needs that initiate the activity. An extremely thirsty individual will exert great effort to find water. Similarly, tremendous efforts on the job often stem from a very high need for achievement.

Effort is usually goal-directed. Thus it can be thought of as the activity or motivated choice that links needs and goals. The concept of expectancy is an important filter. Effort will be expanded only when an individual has reasonable expectation that the goal can be attained. Despite romantic notions to the contrary, the "impossible dream" is not a very real motivating factor.

One main correlate of the concept of expectancy is that blocked goals (perceived or real) will lead to frustration and adaptive behavior. When an individual sees the path to his goal blocked, his reaction most likely will have

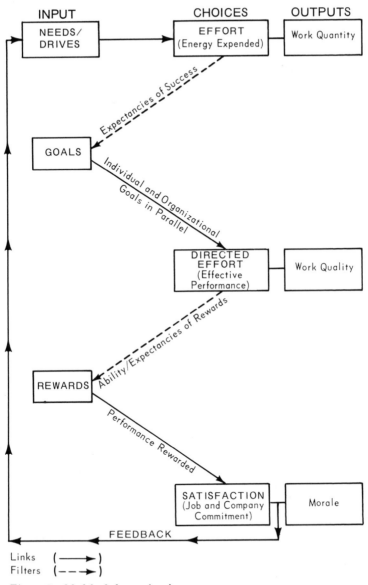

Figure 2. Model of the motivation process.

direct consequences on the organization. The usual reaction to blocked goals tends to be positive:

1. A person will exert extra effort to get past the obstacle.
2. He will evaluate the viability of following another path.
3. He will consider whether other goals might equally satisfy his needs.

Other reactions may be negative:

1. A person may withdraw and leave the need unsatisfied.
2. He may become aggressive and hostile, either to himself or to whatever is blocking his way.
3. He may exhibit other negative reactions often bordering on neurotic behavior.

The main point is that blocked goals lead to redirection of effort. The key operating factor is the person's expectancy that he will be able to attain a particular goal.

Used intelligently, attempts to shape the direction of effort by blocking certain goals can help an organization build an effective motivational climate. But there is always the possibility of producing negative side effects, which will result in frustration. The organization must specify clearly the alternate goals or pathways the employee can pursue to satisfy his needs.

EFFECTIVE PERFORMANCE

The key to work quality is the direction in which effort is expended. The direction is determined by the nature of the rewards available for effective performance. When effective performance is rewarded and ineffective performance is not rewarded or is discouraged by the reward system, high quality work tends to be sustained. As mentioned, when the rewards offered by the organization and the goals of the individual are in close harmony, there is an optimum environment for effective performance and high quality. The direction of effort expended can thus be thought of as a link between goals and rewards.

Management must be concerned with the filters in this link. One is the employee's level of ability. Obviously, unless an individual has the ability to perform his job effectively, no reward system, no matter how extensive, can succeed. The most useful way to view the relationship between performance and ability is to think of performance as a function of motivation multiplied by ability. For example, assume that both motivation and ability can vary on a scale from zero to one. When either motivation or ability is low (equal to zero in our example), their product will equal zero performance. When both are average (.5), performance will be relatively low (.25). When either motivation or ability is high (1.0) and the other only average (.5), performance most likely will be average. And when both are high (1.0), performance will be maximum (1.0).

An employee's expectation that effective performance will be rewarded constitutes another important filter in the link. Unless an individual is sure that his performance will lead to rewards that tie in with his personal goals, he will not choose to direct his efforts toward quality performance. Expectancies of reward supplement the expectancies that filter the needs–goals link.

SATISFACTION

The final link in our motivation system is the satisfaction an individual receives from his job. Satisfaction derives from the rewards given for effective performance and is the basis of employee morale. The level of morale is clearly reflected in the degree of employee commitment both to the job and to the organization.

It is important to understand where satisfaction, or morale, most logically fits into our total motivation system. Not long ago satisfaction was commonly viewed as an *input* to a motivation system like ours and thought to contribute directly to productivity. The general implication was: "A satisfied worker is a productive worker."

When research failed to validate this simple relationship, the concept of job satisfaction per se as a cause of productivity was rethought. It then became clear that it was much more logical to view job satisfaction as an *outcome* deriving from the rewards administered by the organization. Further research substantiated that, most frequently, high levels of effective performance were the *cause* of satisfaction, rather than the other way around. At least this was true when an organization's reward system operated properly. When effective performance was not rewarded or when the rewards did not tie into the goals of employees, no consistent relationship was found between performance and satisfaction. Thus although it still can be said that a satisfied worker is a productive worker, management must recognize that his satisfaction stems from an effective reward system.

Monitoring the System

The link between performance and satisfaction deriving from rewards immediately suggests a novel, extremely useful strategy for monitoring any motivation system. The approach used most frequently in the past was to look directly at the outcome—the morale or satisfaction people expressed about their work and jobs. Various attitude surveys are the commonest techniques for that assessment. Although such surveys provide useful information and have demonstrated their value in a wide range of organizations, there is a more direct way to evaluate a motivation system. That method would look at the correlation between performance and satisfaction within a particular organization unit. When performance and satisfaction are closely related, we can assume that the reward system is functioning effectively. The best performers are the most satisfied, presumably because their performance is consistently rewarded; poor performance is not rewarded, so there is no satisfaction. Thus performance and satisfaction are highly correlated.

On the other hand, the absence of a correlation between performance and satisfaction indicates that something is wrong with the reward system. The better performers are not necessarily getting the greater rewards and therefore are not deriving the greatest satisfaction. High performers and poor performers apparently are receiving equal treatment, so the motivational impact of the reward system is negligible.

FEEDBACK

In our motivation system, as in any system, there is a feedback loop from the output side—satisfaction and morale—to the input factors—needs or drives (Figure 2). When rewarded performance leads to satisfaction, the strength of the need that started the whole process tends to be reduced. Theoretically, since a satisfied need is not a motivator, in a perfectly operating motivational system with perfectly applied rewards tied completely to goals that tie in directly to the needs of the individuals, the system would eventually run down. Needs would be satiated, drives would be reduced, and there would be no force to initiate effort.

But that will not happen. The ideal, perfectly functioning reward system is unobtainable. Rewards will never mesh completely with personal goals; there will never be a perfect link between performance and rewards. No need will ever be completely satiated because, like our need for food, our need for status, for belonging, for challenge, or for more money return regularly.

Further, the hierarchical view of needs discussed earlier suggests that it is impossible to completely satisfy all needs. Even when it is possible to satisfy most of the basic needs, such as needs for security or for pleasant working relationships, higher-level needs are much more complex and much less capable of being satisfied. The highest need in the hierarchy—the need for self-actualization—according to the theory can never be satisfied. When one aspect of a person's potential is realized, new horizons will always open up.

So, while we may think of a satisfied need as not being a motivator, at the same time we recognize that there is no such thing as an unmotivated man. There will always be some unsatisfied needs in all of us. And there will always be some energy driving us toward new goals. The role of the organization is to develop a reward system that channels this effort into desired directions and provides satisfactions that result in commitment to both job and company.

REFERENCES

1. D. McClelland, J. Atkinson, R. Clark, and E. L. Lowell, *The Achievement Motive* (New York: Appleton, 1953).
2. G. H. Hofstede, "The Color of Collars," *Columbia Journal of World Business*, September–October 1972, pp. 72–80.

4

GETTING STARTED

An EMPLOYEE's initial entry into the business world probably is the most critical period in his career. Logic suggests that this is bound to be an important transition, but recent comprehensive research in several large organizations dramatically demonstrates just how important the transition is.[1] The research also suggests that the way an organization provides for a smooth transition for the new recruit, or fails to do so, has pervasive, long-term implications for motivation and productivity—perhaps extending over his entire career. Clearly, these implications are pertinent to our efforts in developing leadership talent for the 1980s.

For most young college graduates today, entry into their first job is as dramatic an event as any they have experienced so far. This step into a career that will last 40 years or more will have a profound impact on the remainder of the young person's life, an impact that probably will be as strong as that of his marriage decision and second only to that of the events that shaped his earlier life.

The new recruit usually sees the job entry process as a rather straightforward transition from dependence to independence. I do not mean just a transition from the traditional financial dependence of youth to the relative financial independence of adulthood; many young people today (although certainly not all) are already financially independent by the time they complete their schooling. The newly recruited manager views his first full-time job more as a transition from dependence for knowledge, for competence, and for leadership, which in past years he has received from his parents, teachers, coaches, and so on. Now he perceives his role as one where he can apply what he has learned, stand on his own, and enter into a position that enables him to exert some influence on the world about him. Although most new recruits have had some work experience, during the summer or on a part-time basis, it is not the same as their first full-time job. Now the new employee expects to be truly independent.

As we shall see, this feeling of newly found independence may in fact lie more in the perceptions of the individual than in objective reality. From both an organizational point of view and his personal psychological point of view, the employee has not yet attained the degree of independence more experienced employees have. The discontinuity between perception and objective fact can cause considerable conflict within the individual. How the organization handles that conflict can determine whether the individual embarks on a successful, highly motivated career or a lackluster parade of mediocre performances.

A recent study I conducted of the career goals of new employees in a large manufacturing organization illustrates vividly the extent to which independence permeates their career expectation. In the study, similar to research carried out in many other organizations, the new employees were asked to rate the importance of well over 50 factors.

Clearly evident among the top factors rated extremely important were items dealing with the desire for personal advancement, job challenge, and adequate training. Some of the needs rated most important were:

> "To feel well trained to carry out your job duties."
> "To feel that your career potential is being adequately developed."
> "To have challenging work, work from which you can get a sense of personal accomplishment."
> "To have a job with variety where you don't always do the same things every day."

Conversely, among the items rated least important were several that reflected dependency, or lack of independence; for example:

> "To work on a job where management provides detailed information regarding how to do your job."
> "To have a job which you can easily perform with your present skills."
> "To have a manager who is able to perform all aspects of your job."
> "To work on a job which requires group effort rather than working independently."

What these new recruits, like new recruits in most organizations today, were saying is that they wanted to stand on their own, provided they had at least the basic training required in order to perform effectively, and to have the opportunity to get ahead through their own efforts. They were entering their careers with a high level of motivation to achieve, a high work orientation and thirst for challenge, and a desire for independence.

ATTITUDE CHANGE

When an individual joins an organization, he very quickly becomes "unfrozen." Many of the traditional forces that have been shaping his behavior, his attitudes, and his values have suddenly been altered. His comfortable equilibrium has been disturbed. The close friendships and easy informality of the university have been replaced by a world of strangers and the hierarchical system of formal business organizations. The flexibility of schedule and rich variety of campus life give way to eight hours a day in an office environment. A move to an unknown city may also be involved. And, most important, the familiar job of going to school, which has occupied his life for almost as long as he can remember, has been replaced by a series of tasks that in some largely unclear way contribute to the broader objectives of his new organization. The transition is very real, and very "unfreezing."

Unfreezing is a necessary forerunner of attitude change. Only when familiar patterns are unfrozen are we ready to change them. It is inevitable that the period of early entry into an organization requires rather strong changes for the new recruit—primarily changes in attitudes and values. There are two major processes by which such changes occur: *identification*, which entails modeling oneself after others and emulating their attitude patterns, and *internalization*, the process by which an individual learns new attitudes and values on his own as a result of being placed in a situation that demands change if he is to function effectively.

Thus the direction of attitude change is a result of both the type of situation the person enters, which demands internalization of the attitude patterns available in the new setting, and the significant other individuals in the environment with whom he may identify—his new peers in pre-management positions as well as his superiors, who serve as role models for the function he will prepare for.

As change occurs and the individual accommodates to the factors that are causing his unfreezing, the process of "refreezing" into the new patterns takes place. At this point, we may say that the person has become socialized into the organization. He has made the transition from the rather stressful position of being an outsider to status as a full-fledged member of the organization. Refreezing results from the individual's efforts to meet the standards or goals of the organization. Obviously, the expectations the organization has for him determine in large measure his degree of satisfaction with the socialization process.

THE SUCCESS SPIRAL

A recent long-term, comprehensive research project demonstrates the critical nature of the socialization process.[2] The research suggested that the individual who meets the performance expectations of his organization and is rewarded will experience deep personal satisfaction if the performance expectations of the organization are reasonably high and mesh with his own level of aspiration. Such satisfaction generally leads to higher levels of aspiration and to an increasingly positive attitude toward the work environment as these expectations continue to be fulfilled and rewarded.

When the individual fails to attain performance objectives that are reasonably high, presumably he will not be rewarded and will experience a sense of failure. As a result, he will tend to lower his level of aspiration, his performance will decrease, and his attitude toward the work environment will become negative.

When routine performance objectives are attained, the individual's motivation and feeling of satisfaction are essentially negligible. Increasing levels of aspiration and internalized high performance standards come only as a result of meeting challenging objectives that test the capability of the individual and pose some chance of failure. Routine performance, rewarded or not, tends to lead only to continued routine performance.

When performance expectations are low, the organization's apparent lack of faith in the individual's ability serves as a blow to his self-esteem. He will respond with dissatisfaction and withdrawal. If even such minimum objectives fail to be met, the employee will tend to blame others.

The combinations of performance expectations and goal attainment show clearly how the pattern of aspiration and satisfaction set early in the job socialization process has long-term implications for career success. The research studies mentioned above tended to substantiate the cause and effect of this process. Successfully meeting high levels of performance standards set during the early period of a new recruit's career led to rewards, increased levels of aspiration, and positive job attitudes. In turn such internalized patterns led to higher levels of performance, which presumably were also rewarded, and led to even more positive attitudes and higher levels of aspiration. In sum, a spiral of success had been set off. It all started with initially challenging, demanding performance expectations that stretched the new recruit.

Conversely, either low performance expectations or the new recruit's failure to meet high expectations will at best be motivationally neutral and at worst deter him from exerting effort toward meeting additional performance objectives. Although it may be possible to break out of this pattern, the individual has been socialized into a pattern where his effort is exerted to achieve only as much or as little as is expected of him; there will be no real satisfaction or challenge in attaining those objectives.

For the employee to break out of the pattern, some dramatic unfreezing and pattern of change will have to be undertaken. Too frequently, research suggests, this just does not happen. So the individual moves through the remainder of his career in large measure stunted, dissatisfied, and alienated. Only rarely is it evident that the basic reason his performance is inferior to that of his cohorts is the nature of the job assignment and the performance expectations set for him early in his career.

THE TYPICAL SOCIALIZING EXPERIENCE

It is sad but true that all too often today's organization fails to capitalize on the potential for initiating the success spiral. Unintentionally or (incredibly) intentionally, organizations that do a superb job of managing most other aspects of their operations leave the orientation and socialization of new employees to more or less take care of itself. This is glaring mismanagement when you consider the care, attention, and money invested in recruiting and hiring new employees and in designing and conducting training and development programs for long-term employees who should have been properly indoctrinated in the first place. The new person seems to be viewed as a static commodity whose intrusion into the smoothly functioning organization is more of a nuisance than anything else.

OH, ARE YOU HERE?

Most men and women entering organizations today run into one or a combination of a relatively limited number of approaches to the indoctrination process. "We forgot you were going to start work so soon" is one approach that is all too prevalent. No preparation whatever has been made for the person. No place has been set aside for him to work, key people who will have an important role in his job are out of town, and no real thought has been given to the specific work he will do. The impact on the new employee is shattering. What a contrast to the tender loving care he received during his recruiting contacts with the company. If nobody even remembered he was coming, he quite logically reasons, he certainly cannot be held in very high esteem. The net effect is for him to begin to turn off before he even has had a chance to turn on.

SINK OR SWIM

Another frequently used approach is to carry the recommendation for providing highly challenging initial assignments and responsibility to the extreme. The recruit is thrown into a job and told to do it. The process may be effective if the individual manages to swim. But it would be even more effective if someone were available to provide at least minimal ongoing guidance and feedback. Another key, of course, is whether his ability to swim is rewarded in any significant fashion. Meaningful rewards are the essential catalyst for triggering the spiral of rising achievement aspirations and increased effort.

The sink or swim approach is devastating to the individual who sinks. With ongoing support and monitoring, including judicious altering of objectives, changes in assignments, timely training and coaching, and so on, this highly de-motivating experience quite possibly can be reversed to give the employee a success experience with net positive outcomes.

CUTTING THE EMPLOYEE DOWN TO SIZE

The third approach to socialization is what Edgar Schein calls the "up-ending experience." [3] Here the intention is to confront the new employee with some jolting experience designed to shake him out of his ways of thinking and beliefs and to acquaint him forcibly with organizational realities. Usually it is a process of cutting him down to size, demonstrating that although he may have a lot of classroom exposure, he is not yet all that capable of coping in the real world. Or the process may be used to convince him that in order to get along in his new environment he has to adopt a more "realistic" approach to problems than he was used to at school. He may be assigned to tasks on which it is impossible to succeed, put on simple projects that are demeaning to his self-image, or shown where the theoretical concepts he learned at the university do not work in a particular business setting.

TRAINING

This approach takes a variety of forms, running all the way from full-time formal classroom training for an extensive period, through a formal program of job rotation and exposure to various functions, to different combinations of formal classroom and on-the-job training.

Generally speaking, formal training does not tend to fit in with the goals and desires of potential managers coming into organizations today. As we have seen, they are oriented primarily toward getting on with their careers, becoming involved in challenging work, and developing a sense of competence and independence. When a specific job calls for specialized knowledge, however, employees are eager for training. In the study mentioned earlier, the employees who ranked "To feel well trained to carry out your job duties" high on the list of 50 job factors substantiate this point. In that organization formal training was essential to involvement in meaningful, challenging work and thus was a highly valued goal. Training per se was viewed as just a step toward the more important goal of carrying out job duties.

Job rotation programs tend to be particularly unattractive to highly motivated potential managers. When trainees are assigned to a department to learn what goes on in that area, there is little opportunity for real involvement in meaningful work, and the individual does not have a perspective of the organization into which he can integrate his observations. The whole process may be viewed as a kind of "holding pattern" that prevents him from getting on with what he really wants to do. Certainly the experience contributes little to launching him into the spiral of increased aspiration and goal attainment that results from solid job achievement.

Each of these typical socializing experiences by itself seems less than optimal for getting the new recruit started properly in his career. Probably no one strategy can be effective for all persons. New recruits bring different needs and objectives to their jobs, they differ in ability, and they enter into different kinds of work situations. Probably the best approach is a highly flexible one that integrates several methods of orientation (with the exception of the "no strategy" approach) and that is tailor-made for each individual.

Leadership—Key to the Success Spiral

Clearly, the first-line supervisor is the critical element in setting high expectations for achievement, providing early job challenge and responsibility, shaping behavior through counseling and support, and providing rewards for goal achievement. I agree with a statement I heard recently that although most top executives have not yet diagnosed the problem, industry's greatest challenge by far is the underdevelopment, underutilization, and ineffective management and use of its most valuable resource—its young managerial and professional talent.

In view of the all-important role of leadership, one would think that new employees would be assigned to the most capable, dedicated, experienced, and versatile managers the organization can find, managers who really would be effective in developing this important resource. Ironically, most often precisely the opposite is the case. First-line supervisors of new professionals tend to be younger men who themselves are just making the transition from professional ranks into management. Usually they are not yet secure in their own position. Typically they have not yet found how to refocus their thinking from "doing" to "managing." As a result they lack the perspective and the maturity to carry out the role necessary for supervising new recruits. On the other hand, new employees may be assigned to old-timers who either have never gotten beyond the first-line position or are on the way back down after reaching their level of incompetence. First-line managerial ranks in all organizations seem to have many individuals who are merely hanging on because there is nowhere else to put them. It is extremely dubious that either new supervisors or jaded managers are the optimal persons to take on the job of socializing new recruits.

The most capable people for filling this crucial leadership role have already moved out of first-line management positions. This suggests, then, that perhaps new premanagerial talent should not be assigned to first-line managers. Rather, senior managers should be asked to take on the developmental role, at least through the new employee's first year. Or, at the very least, there has to be some systematic attention to upgrading first-line managers to execute their training responsibilities more effectively. This means clarifying the importance of the function, outlining some of the roadblocks to the effective socialization of new employees, and training managers in the use of proper indoctrination techniques.

REFERENCES

1. D. E. Berlew and D. T. Hall, "The Socialization of Managers: Effects of Expectations on Performance," *Administrative Science Quarterly*, September 1966.
2. Ibid.
3. E. H. Schein, "How to Break in the College Graduate," *Harvard Business Review*, November–December 1964.

WINDING
DOWN

INTRODUCTION

THERE CAN BE little doubt that the winding down process is widespread in organizations in the 1970s and that much of it starts early in the employee's career. The effects of the motivation crisis are of increasing concern to management. Attitude surveys confirm the crisis. High rates of attrition and absenteeism suggest it. Shoddy workmanship and poor quality reflect lack of commitment. And organizational flexibility and adaptability are hampered by increasing skills obsolescence and redundant personnel who have become passive and have fallen behind in the flow of technology and knowledge. The impact on organizational effectiveness is very real and very expensive.

5
JOB DECAY

WHY HAS THE winding down phenomenon become a crisis? Robert Ford of AT&T implies that it may result from a process of decay in jobs.

> Unless a job has very elastic boundaries and psychological growth and learning can occur, it will eventually bore its incumbents. People, like plants, may need to be repotted occasionally, at least until the pot is big enough for the specimen to grow without stunting. Once we have done our best to make a good and challenging job, the onset of boredom will vary with the ability of the incumbents. For some, the job may be good for a lifetime; for others, only a few years.[1]

Ford's response to job decay is job enrichment —changing the job itself or the kind of work people do to provide more challenge, involvement, identity, sense of achievement, and thus motivation. Job enrichment is a valuable concept, and there has been a great deal of research and experience with it, particularly in recent years. We shall discuss it in more detail in a later chapter.

However, job enrichment seems too simple a solution to the problem of job decay. It says, in effect, "Here is a problem and a solution." It does not pinpoint the cause of the problem, which we must know in order to prevent decay.

Another question is: Why do jobs decay now, in the 1970s, when presumably the problem was not as widespread a few years ago? Is the winding down process a new phenomenon, or has it been present in organizations all along but only now is coming into the spotlight? If it is new, what changes have taken place in industry and society to bring about this crisis?

There are some rather strong reasons to believe that the problem is relatively new. True, industrial jobs 20, 30, 50, or 100 years ago might not have provided high levels of skills utilization, might have been boring, and in terms of content might have been little different from many jobs today. But the industrial environment of the 1970s differs in some rather important aspects from what it was in the past. These differences suggest that the consequences of job decay as evident in the current motivation crisis may be relatively new.

THE CHANGING INDUSTRIAL ENVIRONMENT

We shall discuss some of the obvious areas of differences to provide a perspective. The list is not exhaustive but is designed merely to suggest that there are, in fact, many changes in the industrial environment that undoubtedly contribute to the current problems.

Accelerating pace of society and technology. As Alvin

Toffler so vividly demonstrates in *Future Shock*, the accelerating rate of change in the 1960s and 1970s has had a profound psychological impact on many people.[2] Disorientation, lack of a clear self-perception of job role, psychological stress, and general malaise are much more probable in this environment of explosive change than was the case just a few decades ago. The geometric progression of technology, of course, also contributes to increasing obsolescence of both skills and knowledge as well as to obsolescence of motivation among people who fail to adapt to the changes around them.

Increasing mobility. People are moving about at a rate unheard of just a few years ago. Our society has become used to mobile families, easy travel, long-distance communications, changing employers, changing careers. The element of rootlessness in our society builds a sense of impermanence. We expect things to change—jobs to change or, if not, we will go out and get a different one ourselves. And the new job can just as easily be on the other side of the country as it is in one's hometown. Today norms of many industrial careers are oriented more toward change than they are to permanence, whereas not too many years ago career and job stability and security were most highly prized.

Rising standard of living. We live in a time of unparalleled affluence. One would expect that prevailing norms and goals of most workers, particularly those of young managerial and professional workers, have changed from what they were some decades ago. In less affluent times, people undoubtedly were motivated more by goals somewhat lower in the needs hierarchy than they are now.

There was concern with security, with safety, with making an adequate wage to provide the basic necessities of life, to satisfy social needs of belonging and affiliating with a valued organization.

Today, presumably, most of these needs are pretty well satisfied. Goals and objectives that tie in more with higher-ordered needs for self-esteem, recognition, and sense of achievement have moved into focus. Increasingly, workers take it for granted that their basic needs will be satisfied. They are demanding satisfaction of other needs through their work.

Dramatic increase in levels of education. Today, 25 percent of college-age Americans are enrolled in universities. If the trends of the recent decade continue, it is anticipated that by 1980, 50 percent of college-age Americans will be enrolled.[3] With increasing education come increasing expectations in terms of the jobs that will be filled. Recent experience has shown, however, that very often those expectations cannot be met. We are now in the unheard-of situation of having an oversupply of highly educated people, and the trends probably will become worse in the next decade. This is a sure indicator of probable future underutilization of skills, which will add fuel to the motivation crisis.

Changes in the value systems of young people. Openness and frankness are valued. Immediacy—here and now—rather than deferred gratification is stressed. Life-style and human values have become emphasized, with a relative downgrading of economic and material values. Work is not given the central position in the motivation system that it was some decades ago. With these altered value structures, it is more acceptable to express dissatisfaction with jobs. The dehumanizing aspects of work are particularly vulnerable to criticism. Withdrawing or turning off from an unpleasant or unrewarding situation is a more socially acceptable response than it would have been in the heyday of the work ethic.

Acceptance of protest. People want a better lot in life and are not afraid to say so. We have become so used to the demands for a better deal from all quarters—blacks, women, students, environmentalists, consumers—that individual workers or groups of workers increasingly feel justified in demanding a better return from their jobs.

Rapid growth in size of organizations. In 1950 there were relatively few enterprises in the United States with over $1 billion a year in sales; in 1970 the Fortune 500 showed a dramatic increase. In large organizations there is a tendency toward impersonality. The individual gets lost. He experiences what sociologists call feelings of anomie, or rootlessnesss and lack of identity and purpose. His role and his contributions to the objectives of the giant organization become very unclear. Undoubtedly job decay and winding down tie in directly with growing organizational size.

Routinized jobs. As organizations have grown bigger, jobs have grown smaller. Part of this has been by conscious design. To manage large, complex organizations, managers have instituted various procedures to rationalize and control work. The assembly line is the most obvious example, but the effects have been felt in all work in large organizations—manufacturing, engineering, and development. With technical projects, development is broken down into small modules, clerical jobs are fractionated, and staff functions and management roles are increasingly specialized.

The classic way to control a complex and very large industrial organization is to clearly define the nature of jobs, to specialize them, to break them down into small, readily measurable units, and to standardize work procedures. The heyday of the methods engineers in manufacturing was in the 1930s, 1940s, and 1950s. Production efficiencies were achieved by standardizing jobs and reducing them to the smallest observable, measurable units. The thrust was to take all discretion and individuality out of work. It was efficient, improved productivity, widely applied not just on the factory floor but in administrative and managerial jobs as well. Job shrinkage has been a deliberate management strategy.

New demands from unions. Just a few decades ago, unions were battling management to obtain rewards very basic to the welfare of their constituents. The conflicts were over pay, benefits, and working conditions. Who could be concerned with the kind of work people were doing when the basic conditions of work left so much to be desired? In the 1970s, that battle has largely been won. Labor legislation prescribes basically decent working conditions. Pay is important but nowhere near the issue that it was several decades ago. In fact, probably one of the reasons that unions have experienced little growth over the past decade is that the traditional things they fought for are relatively well taken care of. Workers have not seen how unions can contribute much more.

But now, new concerns are being expressed. There

are indications that unions may be turning onto the issue of the basic satisfactions in work and the winding down process. It is not at all unlikely that during the rest of the 1970s we shall see more and more of the thrust of union negotiations dealing with the nature of jobs and the satisfactions union members can derive from work. Thus there is a very real potential for entirely new dimensions to the collective bargaining process in American industry during the remainder of this decade. These changes, if they occur, will be a direct reflection of differences in the industrial scene between now and the past.

Declining industrial growth rate. It is clear that at least in some industries the growth of organizations, which we outlined before, began to slow down in the late 1960s and early 1970s. For example, the aerospace industries are maturing, if not actually declining. Some of the great growth industries of the 1960s have begun to plateau—computers, semiconductors, airlines, education, and government. There are still vast organizations in these industries, but their growth rates have tapered off. In these circumstances, a slowdown in mobility is inevitable. Advancement opportunities tend to dry up. Whereas in the 1960s people might have been promoted regularly within a period of, say, two years, in a more stable industry job tenure may stretch out to five or even ten years in a single position before a promotion comes along. The process of organizational growth in and of itself tends to prevent job decay. Without it, the potential for decay is much likelier.

For these reasons, as well as for others, it appears that today's industrial environment is a qualitatively different one from what it was some decades ago. The nature of the differences suggests that the motivation crisis and job decay may be relatively new. At least they are new in the sense of their current impact on American industry.

With this in mind, we need to do more than merely say, "Here is a problem, here is a solution (job enrichment), now let's apply the solution." We need to know more about the dynamics of the job decay process. What is it, quite specifically, that feeds into it? Where are the leverage points an organization has to prevent job decay rather than try to counteract it once it has already set in?

What's the Crisis All About?

A recent research project that attempted to clarify the dynamics of declining job satisfaction among several groups of professionals serves as a basis for providing some of the answers to the question "Why?" raised above. The findings lead to a model of attitude change pertinent to the winding down and turning off phenomenon. They also provide some insights into leverage points an organization must apply to prevent job decay.

The research involved detailed analysis of attitude survey results among several large groups of professional employees. Previous research (which will be reviewed in some detail in Chapter 6) had found that certain questions dealing with the individual's intention to stay with the organization or to leave were in fact related to actual attrition for these groups. In other words, this index of commitment to the organization had validity; employees who registered low levels on the index had a high probability of leaving within one year of the attitude survey; those who registered high levels of commitment on the index had a high probability of remaining for at least one year longer. In effect, this survey was found to contain a useful index of how wound down an employee might be, how close he was to actually resigning from the organization. The index thus served as an ideal starting point for a detailed analysis to unravel the factors most associated with winding down.

In this analysis the approach was to use a sample of professional employees who had participated in two different attitude surveys separated by roughly a five-year interval. For this sample, it was possible to identify the individual survey respondents. Therefore it was feasible to compare the attitudes of an individual at time 1 with his attitudes toward identical job components at time 2 five years later. It was also possible to identify the factors that seemed most closely related to declining commitment to stay with the organization as measured by the winding down index.

Each survey contained a large number of questions about attitude. The responses to the two surveys were compared, and a change score for each item for each individual was computed. The change score reflected the difference, in either a positive or a negative direction, between the individual's attitude in a particular area at time 1 as opposed to his attitude five years later at time 2.

With the change scores, it was possible to determine which factors were most closely associated with change in our key indicator of commitment. For example, the analysis evaluated such questions as: "If an individual winds down in overall commitment, does his satisfaction with key aspects of his job (how he views his management, pay, benefits, training, workload, and so on) also wind down?" "For which of these components is the trend most pronounced?" The research also asked: "What can we learn by evaluating those aspects of the job where changes in attitude are *not* related to changes in commitment to stay with the organization?"

An analysis of the answers to the large number of questionnaire items in both surveys enable us to build a model of the winding down process. Because the model fits with more general theoretical positions, and because the major components of the model stand up in analyses of other groups, we shall draw on this research to illustrate what seem to be the major factors in the winding down process.

First, two key elements from the broad array of job-related attitudes seem most closely related to the overall commitment index we have used as our measure of winding down: a general evaluation of the company itself as a place to work and an overall evaluation of the job, the kind of work people do. The analysis suggested that where satisfaction with either of these two components had increased over the five-year period, there was a greater than chance probability that the employee's commitment index had also increased. Conversely, where either had decreased over the five years, there was a greater than chance probability that his commitment index had also decreased. Thus the two components company and job attitudes functioned as major inputs to the winding down process.

For this particular group, it was especially interesting that the trend on the commitment index most often declined over the five-year period, along with the related aspects of company and job satisfaction. The decline bears out the general trend, shown in Figure 1, for job satisfaction to decrease with length of service. However, the analysis that contrasted the attitudes of *individual* employees at time 1 with the attitudes of the *same* individuals at time 2 showed greater declines than would be suggested by a single survey. The two surveys conducted five years apart showed that a significant fraction of the employees who were most dissatisfied at time 1 were no longer available to participate in the survey at time 2. Presumably they had quit their jobs or, if they were marginal performers, perhaps had been released. Thus the remaining group who were still around to participate in the second survey five years later had been among the more satisfied individuals at time 1. The analysis of their individual scores showed large declines in attitudes and a dramatic picture of the winding down process within individuals. As we have indicated, the winding down problem seemed artificially less dramatic in a survey of a total group at one point in time for various seniority groupings. Such analysis of attitude declines for individuals over time, rather than studies of groups at a single point in time, suggests that the winding down problem probably is more serious than many traditional one-shot surveys reveal.

The data for these professionals surveyed five years apart clearly demonstrated that changes in their attitudes toward their companies and toward the kind of work they were doing tied very closely to the winding down phenomenon. The next step was to search for other factors that might tie into winding down.

The analysis showed that in fact other aspects of job attitudes were related to the winding down process, but not as strongly as the two key elements company and job. For example, satisfaction with pay was a likely candidate. General levels of satisfaction with pay for this group of professionals had declined over the five years, paralleling declines in commitment and in people's attitudes toward company and job. It had been expected that declining pay satisfaction might be a major factor in declining commitment—that people who became dissatisfied with their pay would become less "loyal" and therefore more apt to attrit.

As Figure 3 suggests, however, there is clearly no relationship between changes in satisfaction with pay and declining commitment. The figure shows that of those individuals who became more dissatisfied with their pay over the five years 49 percent became more negative about staying. Conversely, 51 percent showed no change or became more positive in their commitment. Of those whose attitude about pay did not change, 35 percent became more negative in their commitment to stay. And of those who became more positive about their pay, 50 percent became more negative in their commitment to stay. In effect, the figure clearly demonstrates that, for this group, changes in people's attitudes toward their pay over five years was in no way related to changes in their commitment index or their winding down.

On the other hand, Figure 4 suggests that there is a direct link between changes in attitudes toward job and changes in level of commitment. None of those whose attitude toward their job increased over the five years declined in commitment; conversely, 31 percent of those

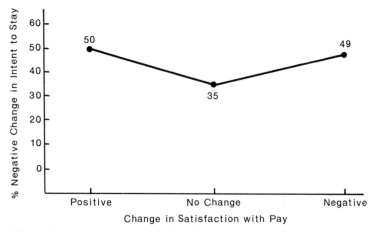

Figure 3. Commitment to stay in relation to pay satisfaction.

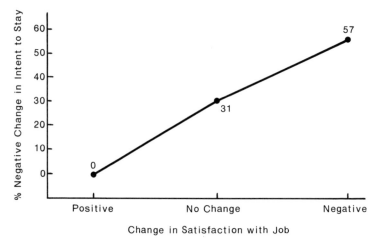

Figure 4. Commitment to stay in relation to job satisfaction.

whose job attitude was unchanged and 57 percent of those whose attitude declined also declined in their commitment to stay. These results suggest that although the decline in intent to stay is independent of the decline in attitude toward pay, it *is* related to the decline in attitude toward job.

The analysis does not suggest that pay is unimportant. It merely says that pay attitudes are not tied *directly* to the commitment index. In the model we shall develop later, it will be clear that pay does feed into commitment, but through a more indirect pattern of attitudes.

Similarly, in this analysis it had been anticipated that work pressure and workload might be related to commitment. The analysis revealed that these factors were unrelated to changes in commitment; there were no suggestions that people quit because of overwork. If anything, as we shall explain, the trend was in the other direction.

On the basis of these findings, we are able to build a model of what seems to be happening in the winding down process. The first part of our model is shown in Figure 5.

The figure shows the two basic attitude components—company and job—feeding into and largely determining the employee's level of commitment. We may think of this as commitment to the company and/or the job, and roughly analogous to the individual's motivation as it applies to his employment relationship.

From the definition of motivation as "a force leading to a choice between alternatives," it is evident that the individual's degree of commitment is behind certain key choices. When commitment is high, one choice is to do a good job, to be productive, to be concerned about quality, to identify with the organization, to be satisfied in the work and work role, to be conscientious, and to be all those "good things" that, in a motivational sense, are the hallmark of a committed, motivated, effective employee.

Another choice—attrition—flows from negative levels of commitment. But here the external environment determines the nature of the choice. Depending on the labor market—the ease with which the individual can get another job—his most obvious choice is to leave the dissatis-

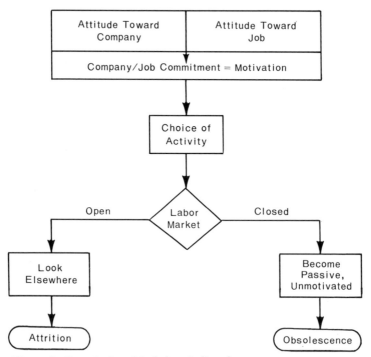

Figure 5. Part 1 of model of the winding down process.

fying environment. We shall discuss this outcome of the winding down process in more detail in the next chapter.

The other negative outcome is probably more serious than direct attrition. This in, in effect, attrition in place, or obsolescence. Here, because the individual in fact or in his pattern of beliefs cannot quit, he hangs on but becomes passive, unmotivated, and dissatisfied. In this situation he very rapidly becomes obsolete. He is no longer contributing as he could or should to the attainment of organizational goals, not to mention his personal goals. In a short time he becomes obsolete in terms of not only motivation but also currency of his skills, abilities, and knowledge. He is a liability, and from the organization's point of view, it probably would have been preferable for him to leave rather than hang on. And from his point of view, obsolescence can be shattering to his self-esteem. We shall discuss obsolescence in more detail later.

The model in Figure 5 now begins to show us where we should concentrate our efforts in the prevention of the winding down phenomenon—on attitudes toward the job and the company. But we still do not have a sharp picture of the dynamics of these two primary attitude areas. What are the factors that really result in satisfaction with the company? And which factors are related most strongly to people's attitudes toward their jobs—the kinds of work they do? Are the components of both attitude areas the same? Here, further analysis of the changes over the five-year period, as well as an examination of other attitude studies and conceptual frameworks from broad-based studies of organizational psychology, help fill the gaps.

ATTITUDE TOWARD COMPANY

In the analysis of survey results, changes in attitudes toward many components of the working relationship were related to changes in attitude toward the company in general. The strongest relationships involved a class of factors we call job context. They may be thought of largely as factors contained in the work environment, or as "context" items:

- Feelings of job security.
- Satisfactory physical working conditions and facilities, such as freedom from excessive noise, a decent cafeteria, proper heating and ventilation.
- Pleasant, harmonious relations with other employees, including both peers and supervisors.
- Satisfactory company programs, such as suggestion programs, social clubs, or communications programs.
- Satisfactory fringe benefits.
- Satisfactory work hours.
- Satisfactory pay.

The common thread of these factors is their usefulness in defining the environment in which the employee works. Interestingly, for this particular group at least, pay functions more as part of the work environment than as an attribute of the work itself. It is one of the factors that sensitize people's attitudes toward the company rather than toward their jobs.

Persons familiar with Herzberg's theory of job satisfaction [4] will see immediately how context factors shape an employee's attitude toward his company. Herzberg says one class of attributes of a job relationship logically can be thought of as organizational hygiene. They are the things found in any progressive, effective organization in today's society. But, Herzberg contends, these attributes—pay, working conditions, interpersonal relations, and so forth— serve only as dissatisfiers, not as motivators. If an organization does not maintain hygiene items at an adequate level, employees will become dissatisfied with their working relationship.

On the other hand, high levels of satisfaction with hygiene factors will not necessarily lead employees to become more productive. Other factors are critical here. At present we take adequate pay, good benefits, decent working conditions, and the like for granted. We are dissatisfied if we do not receive them, but their positive motivational potential is negligible.

JOB CONTENT

In contrast to the factors most closely associated with how people felt about the company, different types of job attributes seemed most related to changes in attitudes toward the kind of work people did. These were changes in how people felt about the *demands* of their jobs, their feeling of having the *ability* to do their jobs, and their view of *growth* opportunities in the organization. The factors to be considered under the category *job demands* include employees' views of—

- The extent to which the job used an individual's skills and abilities.
- The intellectual demands the job made on him.

- The challenge perceived in the job.
- The amount of work expected (with increasing feelings of high work expectations associated with increasing satisfaction with the job).
- The time demands of the job (again, with increasing perceptions of relatively heavy time demands
  associated with increasing job satisfaction).
- The responsibility he perceived the job offered
  him.

In effect, the job demands items from the research findings we examined dealt with the extent to which an individual felt the work he was doing challenged him, stimulated
him, forced him to use his abilities, and in general
required him to expend energy and attention for its completion.

The responses to the survey questions dealing with
the amount of work expected and the time demands of the
job in this constellation of items are particularly interesting.
This group of professionals perceived overwork and high
work pressure as more satisfying than low or limited job
pressure. In effect, not having enough to do is a much
more devastating state of affairs than having too much.
There may be some question whether the trends hold in
quite the same way for nonprofessional groups, but for
these professionals at least this seems to be the case.

The next constellation of factors dealt with ability to
get the job done. This category includes factors in the
working environment that one might think of as belonging
to the context items discussed earlier. In retrospect, however, it is clear that they are related more to attitudes

toward the work itself than to attitudes about the company in general. Among the factors in this category are:

- Having the information needed to do the job.
- Having the authority to carry out the job.
- Having clear job scope and responsibilities (in other words, knowing what the job is supposed to be).
- Feeling qualified to handle the responsibilities.
- Having the necessary training.
- Feeling that there is good teamwork and shared objectives with other persons in the department.
- Relative freedom from unreasonable bureaucratic controls, rules, regulations, and procedures that inhibit the individual's perceived ability to get the job done.

Within the framework of ability to get the job done, we can include all the attributes of a working relationship that directly support and contribute to the successful completion of the task.

A final cluster of attitudes that related more to feelings about the job than about the company in general dealt with growth opportunities, such things as:

- Feeling that past progress in the job has been good.
- Being aware of career opportunities.
- Feeling that the chances of actual promotion are good.
- Feeling that one's personal skills are being developed through the work.
- Feeling that one is learning new things.

For this group of professionals, who were highly advancement-oriented, questions dealing with promotion

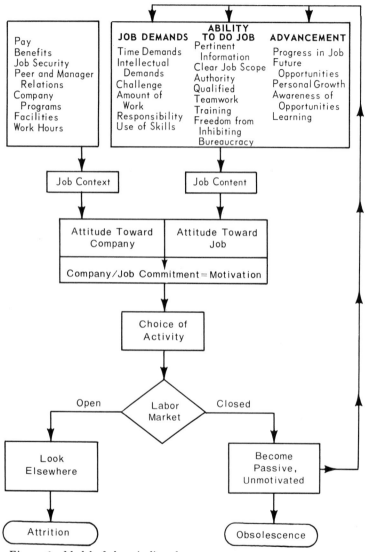

Pay	**JOB DEMANDS**	**ABILITY TO DO JOB**	**ADVANCEMENT**
Benefits	Time Demands	Pertinent	Progress in Job
Job Security	Intellectual	Information	Future
Peer and Manager	Demands	Clear Job Scope	Opportunities
Relations	Challenge	Authority	Personal Growth
Company	Amount of	Qualified	Awareness of
Programs	Work	Teamwork	Opportunities
Facilities	Responsibility	Training	Learning
Work Hours	Use of Skills	Freedom from	
		Inhibiting	
		Bureaucracy	

Job Context Job Content

Attitude Toward Company Attitude Toward Job

Company/Job Commitment = Motivation

Choice of Activity

Labor Market

Open — Look Elsewhere

Closed — Become Passive, Unmotivated

Attrition

Obsolescence

Figure 6. Model of the winding down process.

94

seemed central to this particular cluster of items. It was clear, however, that concern with these items implied more than just the desire for advancement. The participants' attitudes about the kind of work they did were also closely tied in with the extent to which they felt that they were learning new things through their jobs, that their skills were being developed, and that their overall competence was being enhanced by their work. Where these attributes were missing, attitudes toward the job tended to become negative over the five-year period, accompanied by winding down and declining commitment.

In Figure 6, we have added the description of the job context and job content factors into our model of the winding down process. The model rather nicely demonstrates some of the dynamics that seem to occur in the evolution of employee attitudes.

Job context factors can be thought of as primarily sensitizing people's feelings about their company as an employer. When these environmental attributes decay, the company will be less valued as a place to work, and commitment to maintain the employment relationship will decline. Depending on the labor market and the ease of changing jobs, attitude declines will probably lead to attrition. People do leave organizations because of dissatisfaction with their pay or benefits or working conditions. Undeniably, context items are important, and satisfaction with them must be monitored and maintained. But satisfaction with context factors does not mean that winding down can be prevented.

The more potent set of factors for positive job motivation seems to be in the content areas. Here, having enough of the right kind of challenging work, the tools and environmental conditions to support job performance, and an opportunity for enhancing one's personal skills and position through the work are the major inputs to job satisfaction. When these factors begin to decay, job satisfaction will deteriorate and set the winding down process into motion.

In Figure 6, the feedback loop in the job content factors shows that job decay tends to feed on itself. Suppose, for example, the demands of the job decline and one's attitudes go down and motivation begins to decay. This process then feeds back into the other job content factors. The employee begins to become passive and unmotivated and loses any sense of personal growth in his work. As he becomes obsolete, he is increasingly unable to get the job done. These results lead to further declining attitudes about the job, further decay, and increased loss of motivation. A vicious circle sets in. It may be thought of as the negative counterpart of the success spiral initiated early in an employee's career. We suspect that this negative feedback, and demotivation spiral, is largely behind the winding down process and current motivation crisis affecting industry.

Over the past few decades, industry's efforts to combat the winding down process have focused almost exclusively on context items. This has been in response to a combination of factors: labor union pressures, the growing voice of personnel specialists, and early behavioral science research findings. Some of the remedies were chosen because they represent the most tangible, easiest approaches to "morale" problems. As a result, a great deal of emphasis has been placed on insuring pay equity within the organization as well as among similar organizations in the community. The same concern has focused on benefits programs. Communications programs, suggestion programs, social clubs, cafeterias, carpeted offices, and the like have proliferated in management's attempt to bolster sagging job satisfaction. The effect has been, perhaps, an increase in attitudes that say, "Yes, this company is a good place to work." However, the model in Figure 6 suggests that such programs have had very little effect on people's attitudes about their work.

Perhaps part of the emphasis on context has come from the traditional orientation of industrial attitude surveys. Usually they are carried out by personnel people and thus focus very heavily on issues within the area of responsibility of personnel specialists—pay, benefits, communications, and so on. Thus when problems are identified, remedial programs tend to focus on those issues. But our model suggests that much of this concern and action may be viewed as the application of Band-Aids rather than as a real antidote to the winding down process.

On the other hand, concern with content items is relatively new. The job enrichment movement we shall discuss later is one action-oriented outcome of this concern. In its present form, the movement stems directly from Herzberg's theory, which is quite similar to the model in Figure 6. It is in this area—in the issue of job demands, ability to get the job done, and growth opportunities—that organizations will increasingly have to expand their energies if they are going to head off the winding down process.

References

1. Robert N. Ford, *Motivation Through the Work Itself*. AMA, 1969, p. 195.
2. Alvin Toffler, *Future Shock* (New York: Random House, 1970).
3. "The Job Gap for College Graduates in the '70's," *Business Week*, September 23, 1972, pp. 48–58.
4. F. Herzberg, B. Mausner, and B. B. Snyderman, *The Motivation to Work* (New York: Wiley, 1959).

6
WITHDRAWING

For years behavioral science research has been assessing a broad spectrum of factors associated with job attitudes. A great deal of this work has attempted to link morale measures and important factors such as productivity or work quality. Reviews of much of this research usually conclude that, with the exception of one key area, the relationship between morale and performance is complex, and simple generalizations are impossible.

The exception is the organization's ability to maintain its workforce. Study after study has shown that, given a relatively open job market or mobility potential, the extent to which employees withdraw from their jobs—quit or just don't come to work—is related to the degree of satisfaction they derive from their work. When a man is satisfied with his job, rarely will he engage in activities that are detrimental to his company. When he is dissatisfied, he may react by becoming passive, complaining, seeking relief with the help of a third party or union, or committing sabotage. But if possible, he will more likely withdraw from a dissatisfying situation.

In studies of absenteeism it is not uncommon to find job dissatisfaction tied in somewhere as a major factor in attrition. For example, in one organization the absence rates over a six-month period were contrasted for 24 key work departments doing similar work and staffed by similar personnel. An employee attitude survey found that half the departments had high morale and half relatively low morale. Over the six-month period there was a definite trend for the absence rate of the low-morale group to be 60 percent higher than the rate in high-morale departments. The clear inference is that low morale was leading employees to withdraw from the work scene, with significant costs to the organization in the form of reduced efficiency and employment of temporary replacements.

From all indications, absenteeism has reached serious proportions in such chronically dissatisfying jobs as automobile assembly. In some instances production has been delayed for extended periods because key stations were left unmanned. Clearly, the winding down process is crippling production.

Attrition, the other aspect of withdrawal, has received considerable attention. Although the actual attrition rate of recent college graduates may have slowed somewhat following the economic downturn of the early 1970s from a high point in the late 1960s, few personnel specialists feel that the basic problems behind turnover have been reduced significantly. The factors in the external labor market that serve as "pulls" to attrition might be blunted by a depressed economy and reduced mobility potential, but the internal factors serving as "pushes" continue. In all probability, they will grow stronger as the values of young adults are felt more and more in industrial organizations.

The major pushes to attrition include such key factors as frustrated advancement aspirations, feelings of isolation from significant decision making, increasing dissatisfaction with job content, which is often seen as fractionated and lacking in challenge and of limited meaning in relation to the broad problems of society, and growing general restlessness, which finds satisfaction in the act of moving per se. With an actual decline in mobility potential because of a slackening demand for and a growing supply of talent, dissatisfaction and loss of motivation can only increase unless specific actions are taken to counter the pushes.

The extent of the problem of turnover among high-talent personnel was reported in *Fortune*. A 1968 survey found that turnover among managerial and professional employees in a spectrum of major companies reached up to 35 percent a year.[1] The report by most companies that turnover was on the increase substantiated the findings of other studies. A rule of thumb used by many placement people is that at least half the new college graduates entering business will change jobs at least once during the first five years after graduation. Clearly, a high rate of turnover among professional and managerial manpower in American industry is a fact of life.

High Costs of Attrition

Most managers tend to view a high turnover rate with alarm. Their concern usually centers on costs—direct and indirect. The obvious direct costs of attrition are:

1. Hiring a replacement.
2. Training.
3. Salary of the replacement during the nonproductive learning period.
4. Errors and inefficiency during the learning period.

Indirect costs are incurred by:

1. The impact on recruiting when potential hires consider the high attrition rate of their prospective employer.
2. The effects on the morale of present employees when they see their peers, superiors and subordinates leaving.
3. The increased workload and demands on managers who must supervise inexperienced replacements.

We should also mention the toll dissatisfaction takes on an individual, as well as the monetary and emotional costs to the man or woman who changes jobs.

In view of these costs, a persuasive case can be made that any company can realize significant savings through more effective control of attrition. For a large organization, it is not at all difficult to justify a conclusion such as: "For each one percent we are able to cut off of the attrition rate, we will save a half a million dollars!" (or a million, or some other impressive amount).

It would be a serious mistake, however, if we too readily accept this type of accounting as a complete picture of attrition costs. On the contrary, many companies have found that a moderately high rate of attrition, rather than being a liability, should be registered as an asset. For example, attrition, if properly and selectively controlled to see that the right people are staying and the marginal ones leaving, can provide a constant infusion of new blood and fresh, vital thinking, insure a relatively constant availability of high-level talent for movement into managerial ranks, maintain a continuing recruiting demand—through periods of belt tightening as well as prosperity—with concomitant goodwill on the college campus and the efficiencies of a smoothly functioning recruiting machine, and serve as insurance against obsolescence caused by lack of mobility and job change so prevalent in the middle levels of many organizations.

The one sure thing that can be said about the relationship between attrition and organizational success, and thus cost, is that there is no simple relationship. Low turnover may be found in the more aggressively growing organization where the high-talent man finds sufficient job challenge and opportunity, as well as in the stagnant organization staffed by complacent has-beens (or never-will-be's) without the opportunity or the gumption to go somewhere else. Conversely, high attrition may be found in the successful organization that permits and even encourages relatively high controlled attrition, as well as in the formerly successful company coming across hard times. The key for effective management, of course, is to selectively control attrition.

CONTROLLING ATTRITION

Since the costs can be high—of too high a rate of attrition, excessive attrition of the wrong people, or too little attrition—management has a real need to know something about the people who are leaving, why they are leaving, whether their leaving is a net loss or gain for the organization, and where the points of leverage are for exercising managerial control in this important area. The major systematic techniques used for gathering such information are exit interviews, follow-up surveys among employees who have left, and attitude surveys among current employees.

EXIT INTERVIEWS

The exit interview is probably the most typical technique used for assessing terminations. Usually the exit interview has two objectives: (1) to serve as a checkout of the terminating employee to insure that he has returned company property, is aware of his benefits status, and receives his final pay, and (2) to determine his reasons for leaving and learn about the nature of his new job. Sometimes both objectives are pursued during a single interview. Experience suggests, however, that because the objectives are so different the results would be more useful if separate interviews were devoted to each objective. Experience also suggests that the exit interview is probably most effective when conducted by someone other than the departing employee's former manager.

FOLLOW-UP SURVEYS

A number of companies mail a questionnaire to former employees, to either their homes or their new places of employment. The questionnaires may probe for the major reasons a person quit, the degree of importance he attaches to a variety of reasons (work itself, management, compensation, advancement, personal reasons, and so forth), how he feels about his new position in comparison with the one he left. The form usually asks for some description of the new position in terms of level of responsibility, compensation, and type of work.

The standardized format of a structured questionnaire can be very useful in developing data on trends from one period of time to another, in comparing various classifications of former employees, and for looking at former employees' attitudes toward their new position as compared with survey data collected among present employees. A questionnaire is more advantageous than an interview in that it provides a standardized framework in which questions are asked, a format suitable for statistical analysis of the results, and the capability of comparative analyses. It suffers, however, from the possibility of bias from nonresponse on the part of some former employees and the risk of missing important information through reliance on prestructured rather than open-end questions.

Experience with the follow-up survey has found that somewhere between 50 and 70 percent response is typical.[2] This rate is not too different from that found in many general attitude surveys administered to present employees by mail and suggests that the technique probably does not suffer unduly from nonresponse-caused bias. However, a more definitive comparison of responders and nonresponders is necessary to adequately evaluate this issue.

ATTITUDE SURVEYS

A number of studies have found that attitudes expressed by current employees about various areas of job satisfaction are related to turnover. A typical example is a survey conducted among a large group of highly trained professionals in a large manufacturing company.[3] One question asked: "If you have your way, will you be working for the company five years from now?" Following this survey, it was possible to track down each participant at two points in time—within one year of the survey and again after six years—to see if he was still employed and, if not, whether he had left voluntarily or involuntarily. The follow-up showed very clearly that the employees' attitudes during the survey were, in fact, related to their subsequent actions:

1. Of the employees who said they certainly would be with the company in five years, none had voluntarily left within one year of the survey. However, 17 percent had left within six years.
2. Of those who said they probably would remain for five years, 8 percent had left in one year and 32 percent had left within six years.
3. Of those who said they were not sure, 20 percent had left within one year and 44 percent had left within six years.

Very clearly, the participants' responses to the general attitude survey were strongly related to their behavior, at least during the next 12 months. The additional attrition experienced beyond the 12-month point was not strongly related to the original survey responses, though presumably it would have been related to updated survey data.

With this information in hand, it was then possible for the company to evaluate other areas of the survey that related to intention to remain with the company. The analysis highlighted those attitude areas that must be monitored most critically in future surveys in assessing the probability of attrition in this particular organization. Then, if future surveys show erosions in satisfaction in these areas, special action programs to forestall probable increases in attrition would be called for.

This is one, admittedly limited example of how attitude surveys can be used to monitor and control forces contributing to attrition. Many other studies in a range of organizations also suggest a direct link between job satisfaction and turnover. Those studies emphasize the extent to which the attitude survey can be an important tool in attrition control.[4]

RELIABILITY OF EXIT INTERVIEW DATA

The exit interview has traditionally been relied on as the primary vehicle for uncovering reasons for attrition; thus it would seem to be important to assess how good a job it does.

Several studies have attempted to evaluate the accuracy of the exit interview, and the results suggest a fair amount of distortion in the information collected. For example, a comparison of the results of exit interviews among factory employees with the results of a questionnaire subsequently mailed to them found many discrepancies between reasons for termination cited on the questionnaire and those given during the interview.[5] It was also evident that many people tended to clam up in the interview but did state their reasons for resigning on the questionnaire. Significantly the information obtained about reasons for unavoidable terminations, such as pregnancy, moving, health, seemed more accurate (greater agreement between the interview results and the questionnaire results) than was the case with information about avoidable reasons. Either unavoidable reasons were unambiguous and therefore more reliably reported in both the exit interview and the questionnaire, or the data dealing with avoidable reasons were more sensitive and possibly threatening to the respondents and therefore were suppressed during the interview. Perhaps both these effects were responsible for the trends. In any event the study suggested that a considerable amount of distortion occurred in exit interviews conducted by management representatives.

Roughly similar results were obtained in a study conducted among marketing personnel who had left a large national organization. On three separate years, major reasons for termination as recorded during the exit interview were compared with reasons given on a follow-up questionnaire mailed within several months of termination. There was a consistent tendency for the exit interview report to overemphasize the importance of personal reasons and dissatisfaction with the work and to underemphasize the desire for autonomy and freedom of action. The results further underscore the difficulty of obtaining accurate information about reasons for termination through exit interviews conducted by management representatives.

One company recently undertook a study to see if more objective information could be obtained from the exit interview. Management recognized the potential for a certain amount of bias in termination information collected by its representatives. To assess the extent of the bias, the company engaged an outside consultant to re-interview former employees. The consultant contacted a random sample of individuals within several months of termination and interviewed them for several hours. Because of assurances of confidentiality and because of the objective viewpoint of the consultant and his interviewing skills, the sessions yielded extensive information about why people were leaving the organization and some penetrating insights into problem areas that had to be addressed in an attrition control program.

An interesting side analysis of the project was a comparison of the information gained from the consultant's interviews and the information gained previously through the company's usual exit interviews. The comparison showed some rather marked discrepancies in the reasons for termination between the two different methods of data collection. Clearly the company was not obtaining a full factual picture of the underlying causes of attrition through its normal exit interview procedures.[6]

These and other studies suggest that in addition to providing relatively inaccurate information, often the exit interview is an uncomfortable, dissatisfying experience for the departing employee, particularly when it is conducted by management representatives. There are a number of reasons for this.

First, the terminating employee probably is reluctant to be honest. He does not want to burn any bridges behind him, recognizing that he may want to return to the company, he may need employment references, or in his new business he may have contact with representatives of his former company. Frequently, he does not want to get his former associates into trouble if they were involved in any way in his dissatisfaction and decision to leave. Also, he probably holds back because he thinks it is in good taste or because he finds it much easier to let sleeping dogs lie.

For many terminees there probably is a considerable amount of rationalization as they compare their new position with their former one. Whereas they can weigh the pluses and minuses of both while they are going through the decision-making process, once the decision is made, the issues seem to become clear. This is the "cognitive dissonance" phenomenon discussed in Chapter 2. The tendency is for most aspects of the new position to be evaluated positively and the old position to polarize as negative. There is also a tendency for conscious or unconscious justification of the important decision to leave, with some inevitable distortion in the individual's recollection of the decision-making process.

In addition, the exit interviewer usually is not completely objective, particularly if he is a representative of management. Very frequently he lacks skill and training in interviewing. His perception of what the employee is saying probably is subject to a certain amount of distortion, both conscious and unconscious, because of natural defensiveness and personal involvement in the circumstances leading to the resignation.

When the objectives of gathering information and

checking out the departing employee are combined in a single interview, the information-gathering objectives probably suffer and render the interview ineffective.

Implications for Management

Current experiences and an evaluation of the procedures industry uses to understand attrition suggest a need for new approaches to the problem. Specifically, there clearly is a need for more reliable information about employees' reasons for leaving a particular organization. The effectiveness of the exit interview should be evaluated; if it is going to be continued, there probably should be training for the interviewers. Interviewing should be centralized and carried out by personnel department staff members (or better yet, by outside consultants) rather than by operating management. And the interview for evaluating reasons for termination should be separated from the interview designed for checking out the employee.

On a broader scale, there is a need to systematically evaluate the costs involved in attrition as a basis for deciding how to selectively control it. Possibly such an evaluation will show that there is not enough attrition in a particular organization; on the other hand, it is quite likely that a program of selective attrition control would be called for.

There probably are two basic elements to a working program for attrition control: (1) an effective system for performance feedback and equitable rewards tied to performance and (2) systematic attention to mobility inside the organization and concern with providing challenging job content so that the high-potential individual does not have to turn outside to satisfy his needs for achievement, personal growth, and development of competence.

A reward system is designed to tell an employee where he stands. The high-potential employee should know both from direct communication and from rewards that clearly differentiate him from average performers that he has a promising future with the company. Conversely, candid feedback to the mediocre employee is only fair and may nudge him into a job change or a performance change that could salvage an otherwise lackluster career. Of course, the degree of candor used with the acceptable but not outstanding employee will vary with attrition experience and manpower requirements. As a generalization, however, there probably is too little candor in the feedback and reward system in most organizations.

Concern with personal growth and challenging job content is the cornerstone of effective manpower utilization. It should be a key element of any company's personnel policy, not simply a means of controlling attrition. Talented and educated manpower is just too important for running today's organizations, and just too expensive to underutilize. But effective utilization becomes even more critical when attrition tends to be high, and is essential for holding the high-potential employee who is vital to future organizational success.

REFERENCES

1. Robert C. Albrook, "Why It's Harder to Keep Good Executives," *Fortune*, November 1968, pp. 136–139, 178–180.

2. Joel Lefkowitz and Myron L. Katz, "Validity of Exit Interviews," *Personnel Psychology*, Winter 1969, pp. 445–456; Julius Yomman, "Following Up on Terminations: An Alternative to the Exit Interview," *Personnel*, July/August 1965, pp. 51–55.

3. A. I. Kraut, "The Predication of Turnover by Employee Attitudes," paper presented at American Psychological Association Meeting, Miami, Fla., September 1970.

4. Allen J. Schuh, "The Predictability of Employee Tenure: A Review of the Literature," *Personnel Psychology*, Summer 1967, pp. 133–152; Victor H. Vroom, *Work and Motivation* (New York: Wiley, 1964), pp. 175–178.

5. Lefkowitz and Katz, op. cit., p. 454.

6. John R. Hinrichs, "Employees Coming and Going: The Exit Interview," *Personnel*, January/February 1971, pp. 30–35.

7
OBSOLESCENCE

WHILE MOST ATTENTION in business has focused on attrition, obsolescence is undoubtedly just as prevalent and just as serious, if not more so. It is a much more difficult problem for an organization to deal with, difficult to identify and difficult to correct.

Obsolescence in an organization is like a cancer. Unless arrested, it will only spread, eventually crippling the ability of the enterprise to adapt to today's volatile business environment and to survive. With the stakes so high, it is imperative to understand what obsolescence is and where it comes from.

THE NATURE OF OBSOLESCENCE

As outlined earlier, a useful way to think of obsolescence in organizations is as attrition in place. In effect, the obsolescent employee might just as well not be there. His performance fails to make a meaningful contribution to the goals of the enterprise. Either he is nonproductive—he just does not exert significant energy on his job—or he is counterproductive—what he does do at best makes no contribution to and at worst detracts from the organization's effectiveness.

Attrition in place suggests two primary dimensions of obsolescence: lack of motivation to perform effectively and lack of skills required to do the job. These two dimensions often interact. As job motivation erodes, the incentive to maintain and update one's skills often erodes as well. And as job requirements outgrow the skill levels of job incumbents—a fact of life particularly prevalent in high-technology industries—performance declines and motivation wanes. We must consider both the motivation and the skill dimensions of obsolescence.

In the middle levels of many organizations—not to mention the top and bottom levels—the careful observer will see far too many individuals who fit the pattern of ineffective performance. These are people who have lost their motivation to perform; they have wound down and turned off where they are. Or they are individuals who never were particularly job-motivated, but who have found a secure shelter in the bureaucratic world. Or they are people who have failed to keep abreast of changing technology and technique. Or, finally, they may be people who have been overpromoted; they have risen to their level of incompetence, fulfilling the prophecy of the Peter Principle: "In a hierarchy, each employee tends to rise to the level of his incompetence. Every post tends to be occupied by an employee incompetent to execute its duties." [1]

Ineffective personnel are mainly found in large bureaucratic organizations where their ineffectiveness can be hidden in legions of staff and routinized procedures. They also are found in smaller organizations, but their ineffectiveness undoubtedly comes to light more readily because there is less possibility for it to be hidden or tolerated.

Ineffective manpower is an issue that too often in the past has not been faced squarely and dealt with constructively. Only rarely has it been recognized as a problem entailing great costs both to the organization and to the individual.

There probably are several reasons for this. First, obsolescence is embarrassing. It is tainted with overtones of failure and tends to run counter to the American dream. Second, it is hard to identify. Just how ineffective does an individual have to be to warrant special attention? What is the boundary between acceptable and unacceptable performance?

As a result, most companies in the past have not taken a constructive approach to obsolescence by upgrading the man whose job skills decay or restoring the motivation of the individual who has lost it. Instead, the tendency is to take the easy solution—to demote the individual, transfer him to a relatively insensitive position (that is, shelve him), or fire him.

A study of current practices indicates that removal from the job in some such way is the usual response to ineffective performance, at least in the case of management personnel.

> When a manager in a key situation is not performing up to the requirements of that position, removal action is initiated by the company if the situation is considered serious

enough to offer a significant threat to the reputation, performance, or future prospects of the business. In most of the firms studied, this phase of the decision is made dispassionately and without compromise. Personnel and human relations factors do not play a significant role at this stage. Thus, once the situation goes beyond tolerable boundaries, the trouble is treated by surgery, not by therapy.[2]

Over the last decade or two, however, obsolescence has become more and more a topic of management concern. There probably are two basic factors behind this emerging trend: the extreme state of environmental flux of contemporary organizations and the proliferation of specialized knowledge.

The impact on organizational effectiveness of the extreme state of environmental flux was highlighted in the turbulent 1960s. Today it is evident everywhere in our society, in the increasing complexity of current technologies and organizations, and in the many ambiguities faced by decision makers. High levels of skills, broad perspectives, flexibility, and competence in the appropriate technology constitute the hallmark of the successful enterprise today. The need for concerted attention to the prevention of personnel obsolescence has come into prominence.

The proliferation of knowledge has been well documented by many impressive statistics showing the geometric progression of literature, research, and professional and scientific manpower. Like environmental flux, the proliferation of knowledge points to the need for continual professional and technical updating to prevent obsolescence.

When one looks at the research studies and general management literature, however, it is clear that if we are to combat obsolescence, we need to know a great deal more about it. For one thing, we need a clearer understanding of just what it is we are dealing with.

Most frequently either of two basic reference points seem to be used in defining or describing the obsolescence phenomenon: the performance of the individual within a specified work role or the degree to which specialized knowledge is lacking in or is unavailable to the individual.

Concern with obsolescence in the framework of the work role has suggested three types of obsolescence: [3]

Professional obsolescence, which results from the discrepancy between an individual's knowledge of his discipline and the total actual knowledge available to professionals in the discipline.

Areal obsolescence, which results from the discrepancy between knowledge in a specialized area of the field and the total existing knowledge for that area.

Ex-officio obsolescence, which results from the discrepancy between the individual's knowledge and the knowledge essential for effectiveness in his position.

The difficulty with such definitions is that they focus on the problems that result from the phenomenon (the symptoms of obsolescent behavior); it is practically impossible to specify just what the individual should be compared with.

The second reference point for describing obsolescence is specialized knowledge per se without regard for its relationship to a specific work role. One approach views in absolute terms the extent of knowledge the individual has of his current field (as an indicator of retention of previously held knowledge), as well as his familiarity with emerging areas of knowledge. This approach, however, does not consider the dynamics of behavioral factors, such as attitudes or motivation, that may be critical in understanding why an individual possesses the required knowledge but still performs in an obsolescent fashion.

At a conference on occupational obsolescence none of the participants was able to formulate a concise definition that was universally accepted by the other participants.[4] Several key factors associated with the concept were outlined.

Change. There is some change in status or movement toward becoming obsolete. Either the individual changes, or the environment changes. The key point is that there is a negative change in the behavior of the individual in comparison with appropriate behavior for his work role.

Ineffectiveness. The change is in the direction of lowered performance effectiveness.

Variety of components. Obsolescence may refer to the status of such things as attitude, knowledge, motivation, behavioral style, or a variety of activities. A specific individual probably would not be obsolete in all characteristics at once but may show varying degrees of obsolescence in each.

Interaction between the environment and the individual. What is obsolescent behavior in one situation may not be in another; an individual may be obsolete in his work role but effective in his total life situation.

From a practical point of view, a firm, cleanly written, commonly accepted definition of obsolescence is not necessary. We may think of obsolescence as ineffective performance that is capable of being corrected. In addition, we shall limit our area of concern to the workplace; obsolescent behavior in an individual's avocations or personal life are beyond our area of concern.

Causes of Obsolescence

We may think of two basic sources of obsolescence that tend to interact: factors in the work role and characteristics of the individual. Factors in the work role contributing to obsolescence are most readily observed in technology-based organizations, although they certainly are found in other organizations as well. They result from some discrepancy between the ability or knowledge requirements of the job and levels of knowledge or ability of individual organization members, so that the resulting discrepancy leads to obsolescent behavior.

WORK ROLE FACTORS

A number of research studies have investigated several attributes that might be thought of as candidates for major causes of work role obsolescence.

Misplacement of personnel. Several studies have highlighted the strong possibility that much obsolescence occurs because the individual was not selected or placed properly in the first place. Misplacement is the core of the Peter Principle. Comprehensive analysis of data from a broad study of American engineers suggests that in R&D organizations, individuals with the greatest deterioration of technical knowledge tend to move into administration, so that technical obsolescence is increased.[5] Clearly, mismatching people and job requirements is a sure way of planting the seeds of obsolescence in any organization.

Inability to keep up with technology. Here, technology advances faster than the person's capability to handle it. Although research suggests that industries characterized by rapid technological change tend to have fewer obsolescent engineers than more stable industries, failure to keep up with changing technology clearly can be an important cause of obsolescence.

Underutilization of skills. When skills are underutilized, as suggested by the widespread indications of a motivation crisis in many organizations today, we may expect obsolescence to occur simply from atrophy of skills. But more important, obsolescence occurs from some of the motivational correlates of underutilization that we have discussed—general lack of interest in and commitment to the job, alienation, focusing on other sources of gratification, and so forth.

Strong trends show that one factor—level of technical responsibility among engineers—is negatively related to obsolescence. In all probability, being responsible for technology forces one to keep up to date, although it is equally plausible that the most up-to-date engineers are assigned high levels of technical responsibility.

In the research done so far, several aspects of the work role were found to be unrelated to obsolescence, contrary to what one might expect. For example, in the study of engineers there was no clear relationship between obsolescence and level of supervisory responsibility. Higher management did not appear to differ from first-line supervision in the incidence of obsolescence, despite their longer time away from purely technical work. Similarly, there was no evidence of a relationship between frequency of exposure to technical and professional colleagues and freedom from obsolescence. Mere exposure to other professionals does not seem adequate for the maintenance of technical skills.

CHARACTERISTICS OF THE INDIVIDUAL

Age. A great deal of research has been devoted to the impact of aging on skill and ability levels. For example, one comprehensive analysis suggests that most highly creative contributions are made by relatively young persons. The analysis does not show, however, that this is a universal, absolute relationship; many examples exist of outstandingly creative contributions by very senior citizens.[6]

Research does suggest that some changes in individual skill levels are a direct function of the aging process. In particular, specific sensory and motor skills tend to peak at some relatively early age and decline thereafter. Research often identifies similar trends in cognitive skills—learning, memory, intelligence, concept formation, and creativity. But the specific aspects of the trends and, in fact, their basic validity are still subject to a certain amount of controversy among researchers.

For purposes of preventing and correcting skills obsolescence, it probably would be safe to say that abilities do decline with age (but not uniformly for all abilities and not uniformly for all people). However, decrements in ability often can be compensated for by increased motivation. Skills can be maintained through use. In addition, other factors, such as greater accuracy, attention to detail, or reliability, are often correlated with aging. Increases in these attributes tend to offset any ability decrements and prevent a specific individual from becoming obsolete within a specific work role.

Other effects of aging quite frequently associated with obsolescence stem from the psychological stress of middle age. There have been several reviews of the diverse sources of such stress and the implications for managerial effectiveness of changes in work style, point of view, family relationships, and personal goals. Maladaptation to such changes can be strongly associated with obsolescent behavior.

Education. Educational background seems to have an important impact on obsolescence. Research among engineers indicated that level of initial education, particularly at the Ph.D. level, tends to be associated with a high level of knowledge of emerging fields and freedom from obsolescence. Research also suggests a correlation between obsolescence of technical skills and length of time since completion of schooling. The picture varies depending on the specific field of knowledge involved.

Motivation. Chapter 5 presented a detailed model of how the winding down of motivation often leads to obsolescence. The problem becomes particularly critical when the job requires high levels of technical or professional skills. There is little doubt that a major factor behind much skills obsolescence is the employee's lack of motivation to keep himself up to date. A recent symposium high-lighted why the motivation to keep up to date is especially important for the prevention of obsolescence, but why at the same time it is very difficult for motivation to be sustained.[7] For example:

> Updating usually is not project-specific; the objectives frequently are very general, vague, and of unclear relevance to present-day work problems.
>
> In most organizations, the rewards for updating behavior are less clear-cut than other rewards for immediate work performance.
>
> The updating process is never-ending and is rarely accompanied by satisfaction from a sense of closure following project completion.
>
> Most updating has to be self-initiated, and it is difficult to maintain self-motivation in the absence of rewards and clearly defined needs.[8]

Skills obsolescence from loss of motivation may be related to age. The job incumbent simply runs out of steam and fails to exert effort to maintain his currency. But usually the implications are broader. Generally some element of job decay and winding down has been allowed to set in. For almost all jobs, as we have seen, after five years or so in one assignment, job requirements are completely mastered and the work itself is no longer motivating. Gellerman makes the point nicely in stating: "The problem of competence loss is to avoid letting too many people learn their jobs too well." [9] For understanding the motivational aspects of obsolescence, somewhere we have to get back to our basic model of the winding down process covered in Chapter 5.

Identifying, Preventing, and Correcting Obsolescence

In the face of increasing incidence and cost there is a growing need for reliable and effective methodologies for combating obsolescence in organizations. One of the most pressing needs is for better techniques and approaches for identifying at the individual and the organizational levels specific areas of obsolescence. This means identifying individuals who have become or are becoming obsolete, whole departments or functions of organizations that have become ineffective, or specific jobs or procedures that need updating. Without reliable identification it is doubtful that appropriate strategies for correcting obsolescence can be developed. At present, however, such tailor-made techniques to identify obsolescence unfortunately are not available.

Some emerging methodologies and strategies do have considerable promise for preventing and correcting obsolescence. As experience with them grows, new and better techniques for identifying obsolescence will no doubt also emerge. We shall discuss these methodologies in some detail later. But first a few specific points about the identification, prevention, and correction of obsolescence are appropriate.

Although little in the research or management literature deals specifically with identifying obsolescent behavior in organizations, obviously the standard evaluation tools of organizations apply: appraisal and counseling programs, management by objectives, ability testing, situation-based skills assessment procedures, and various indicators such as turnover or absenteeism. Periodic surveys of technical and professional employees are a valuable technique for assessing updating needs and educational requirements. And various self-assessment or peer assessment procedures and objective testing might usefully be tried.

Aside from techniques, however, the main thing that is needed to get at the identification and correction of obsolescence is for organizations to admit that the problem exists. Then the standard tools of good personnel management can be very useful in identifying where the problem exists. As pointed out, all too often the problem has been swept under the rug until it is too late: then it is handled "surgically" rather than therapeutically.

In the future, industrial organizations will have to assume a different attitude toward ineffective manpower because the problem will almost certainly become more widespread. With the rapid change characteristic of industry now and undoubtedly in the immediate future, obsolescence will become more probable. Also, with talent becoming more and more critical to organizational success, there will be less and less leeway for the marginal performer in critical positions. There will need to be open recognition of the dangers of obsolescence, overpromotion, and loss of motivation and a willingness to face them constructively to avoid the tremendous losses that will result if the "obvious" quick solution of reassignment is used exclusively.

First of all, this solution is too costly. The expense of finding, developing, and breaking in replacement skills can be far heavier than that involved in upgrading potentially salvageable skills and talents. Second, removal tends to compound rather than solve the problem. Inevitably, such a blow to the individual entails the need for adjustment and a forced change of direction in his career orientation. It precipitates loss of motivation and when it is abrupt—as traditionally such removal has been—it tends to make the marginal performer even more ineffective.

What, in contrast, does a constructive approach to the prevention or correction of obsolescence involve? Several strategies may be of use, singly or in various combinations.

Judicious selection and placement. One writer contends: "Here is where a large proportion of the professional obsolescence can be identified. Put a person in a field wrong for him, in which he has neither the interest nor the talent for success, and you can almost guarantee an abundance of obsolescence not too many years after he enters the job market." [10] In addition to various counseling and guidance procedures and testing programs designed for the proper selection and placement of personnel, the assessment center method has some potential for the differential placement of management personnel. This procedure, which will be described in more detail in another chapter, consists of several days of testing and standardized situational exercises in which the behavior of participants is systematically observed and evaluated. The final outcome is an overall assessment of the optimal placement for each individual. Perhaps this technique should be considered a means to counteract the Peter Principle.

From the point of view of selection and placement, there may be some positive aspect of the obsolescence phenomenon. It is at least conceivable that increasing obsolescence may be sufficient to push a misplaced individual into a mid-career change of profession when obvious misplacement or declining motivation signals the need for something different. Many writers suggest that increasingly careers will be multifaceted rather than homogeneous throughout the work life span. Perhaps obsolescence as we have defined it in this chapter will be one of the signals frequently used in determining the need for such career changes.

Training and retraining. Training is an obvious method for preventing and correcting obsolescence, and we shall discuss it further later. As we have already pointed out, however, the level of initial technical training seems to have some relationship to subsequent obsolescence throughout a career. To prevent obsolescence, organizations increasingly will have to view careers as a series of interludes between education and work so that skills and knowledge are continually upgraded and shaped appropriately for job requirements.

For general ineffectiveness there may be merit in special courses and programs for marginal performers. A company considering such special courses should be very careful to see that there is no stigma attached to participation in them. The company must also insure that training courses made up solely of obsolete people do not turn into a case of the lame leading the halt.

There has been surprisingly little research on the concept of retraining, most of it being limited to blue collar occupations. We need to know more about it—what skills are retrainable, how to retrain, and so forth. We may think of retraining as providing new skills for groups of employees or individuals who have been made obsolescent by technological change. Research suggests that with appropriate program design it is possible to upgrade the skills of employees who ordinarily would be deemed to be marginally trainable. The key factor in the success of a retraining program seems to be largely motivation and revolves around the self-image of the trainee and his confidence that he can succeed in such a program.

Individual development programs. Probably the most useful strategy for combating obsolescence is individual attention through the normal employee-manager relationship. What is needed is an appraisal process capable of identifying problem cases and taking remedial action before they become unsalvageable.

Goal setting and coaching are important in working with the man or woman to improve performance, upgrade skills, and define targets and standards. It is the manager's responsibility to insure that his performance expectations and evaluations of the individual's achievements are brought out into the open.

Job rotation should be used positively to counteract obsolescence, not merely to remove the individual from the job in which he is performing marginally. Rotation should be planned to obtain maximum personal development for him and better utilization of his particular skills. Often, poor performance is a result of interaction with a specific environment. A new boss, a new set of job requirements, or a new job location may be all that is needed to bring the marginal performer up to standard.

Skills utilization. To any organization, full utilization of skills should make sense in terms of simply obtaining appropriate return in productivity on salaries paid. As we have previously discussed, however, all indications are that skills are underutilized to an alarming degree in American industry, and the problem is getting worse rather than better. The whole job enrichment movement is clearly a response to the indications of skills underutilization. Job enrichment may be thought of as a strategy for the prevention of obsolescence as well as a strategy for maintaining motivation and job satisfaction. We shall discuss it in detail later.

In Chapter 4 we discussed how the challenge of the work and the degree of skills utilization during the employee's first few months in the workforce are extremely important in determining his subsequent level of motivation and productivity. Presumably, underutilization of skills early in an employee's career sets off a spiral of lack of motivation, dissatisfaction, and relatively low productivity, which can persist throughout the career. The implications are clear that full utilization of skills, particularly early in the career, is critical to effective current performance and presumably to motivation for updating.

Fostering motivation for updating. A number of key factors must be considered in enhancing motivation for updating.

It must be clearly demonstrated to the employee that his effort will help him maintain effective performance. That is, expectancies that his efforts will be successful have to be built up. This seems particularly crucial in retraining older workers.

The task has to be cut down to manageable dimensions and pieces.

Obtainable, identifiable subgoals for updating should be set for each individual.

Organizational emphasis, demonstrated by organizational practice, should show that updating is an important activity. Few people will exert the considerable effort required unless "somebody up there cares." This means the formal allocation of funds and time for updating activity, policies encouraging self-study or training, and communications programs emphasizing the individual employee's ultimate responsibility for maintaining his own competence.

The reward value of updating behavior should be enhanced by tying it to other, more obvious organizational rewards such as promotion and salary. There must be some expectation that successful effort will pay off.

The major thrust of these motivational points is that updating must be presented as an important organizational objective. If it is not seen as important, creeping obsolescence is just about inevitable.

Surgery. This point must be kept in perspective. We are not saying that an organization should never demote or fire an employee who is performing ineffectively. Sometimes demotion is in his best interests as well as the organization's. An overpromoted manager may actually be thankful to get out of a stressful situation where he realizes he is in over his head. But demotion should not be the only solution, as it is in so many companies today. Individual attention aimed at upgrading and salvage should be tried first.

As for release, generally that should be a last resort. Yet it, too, may be the only solution for both individual and company. At the same time there is a responsibility to the organization, to the individual, and to society as a whole that should be recognized. This responsibility grows in direct relationship to the length of time the person has been employed. Yet when release is the only solution for a severe obsolescence problem, an enlightened organization at least should fix the blame where it belongs—on its own failure to implement countermeasures against the winding down process.

REFERENCES

1. L. J. Peter and R. Hull, *The Peter Principle* (New York: William Morrow & Co., 1969).
2. Graduate School of Business, Stanford University, *Top Management Looks at Loss of Motivation, Overpromotion, Manager Obsolescence* (Stanford, Calif.: Stanford University, 1961), p. 73.
3. T. N. Ferdinand, "On the Obsolescence of Scientists and Engineers," *American Scientist*, 54, 1966, pp. 46–56.
4. J. G. Roney, Jr., *Report on First Conference on Occupational Obsolescence* (Menlo Park, Calif.: Stanford Research Institute, 1966).
5. R. A. Rothman and R. Perrucci, "Organizational Careers and Professional Expertise," *Administrative Science Quarterly*, September 1970, pp. 282–293.
6. H. C. Lehman, *Age and Achievement* (Princeton, N.J.: Princeton University Press, 1953).
7. S. S. Dubin (chairman), *Symposium on Motivation for Professional Updating*, presented at XVII International Congress of Applied Psychology, Liége, Belgium, 1971.
8. J. R. Hinrichs, "Applying Motivational Concepts to Updating," presented

at Symposium on Motivation for Professional Updating, XVII International Congress of Applied Psychology, Liége, Belgium, 1971.

9. S. W. Gellerman, "Competence Loss," Chapter 8 in *Management by Motivation*, AMA, 1968.

10. R. Perloff, "Educational Inhibitors and Facilitators of Professional Updating," presented at Symposium on Motivation for Professional Updating, XVII International Congress of Applied Psychology, Liége, Belgium, 1971.

WINDING
UP

INTRODUCTION

OUR DISCUSSION of the contemporary national scene seems to suggest that job decay is just about inevitable. One might infer that there is a natural process of declining motivation with the simple passage of time. At best, an organization might slow down the decay process; at worst, it must accept the fact and live passively with it.

For many persons working in today's industrial environment, job decay probably is inevitable. Certainly the pervasive signs of turning off in industry suggest that it is true, at least to some extent. Attrition and turnover speak to this—if an organization cannot prevent the winding down process, the individual himself often takes steps to counteract it.

It is clear, however, that much can be done to prevent job decay. Some of these things are new, but some are as old as the basic principles of good personnel management. For many years now, a great deal has been known about the theory and practice of personnel relations in organizations, and this theory and practice continue to be applied with varying degrees of sophistication and varying degrees of success, in today's organizations. For example:

Manpower planning that attempts to insure the right types of skill of the right degree and the needed amount of skill units in the right places at the right times, performing activities necessary to the vitality of the organization, can go a long way in preventing job decay. Certainly, if plans match reality and fulfill all these objectives, and if they are carried out, there should be few people in jobs that do not match their level of skill. The problem, however, is that most often there is a big gap between planning and action.

The traditional personnel activities of recruitment, selection, and personnel placement, if executed effectively, will also insure that job requirements match people requirements, so that the motivational potential of jobs is maximized.

Job evaluation procedures are designed to insure equitable payment based on duties performed and appropriate recognition for differences in contributions to organizational objectives. Effective job evaluation is an important factor in preventing job decay.

Compensation systems, under which we include both salary administration and the application of fringe benefits, if operating properly should provide tangible rewards for effective job performance and thus be an important input to the motivation system.

Effective recognition programs also should contribute to the motivation system. These include special awards, attention to the individual, contests, as well as status perquisites like titles and special facilities. Enlightened managements include such recognition programs in their personnel functions.

Communications programs obviously are important for maintaining job motivation, including everyday management communications practices, adequate channels that employees feel will provide a fair hearing for their grievances, and more formal communications channels such as newspapers, bulletins, and postings.

Adequate physical working facilities, such as lighting, ventilation, equipment, and space, are vital to employee motivation.

The last but certainly not the least important component of effective personnel policy is adequate attention to the human relations aspect in the work environment. People must be treated as human beings and must be assured of management's genuine commitment to building as much job satisfaction and security into the working relationship as possible.

All these basic personnel practices, of course, are very important in preventing job decay. They can be thought of as a base for sustained commitment both to the job and to the company. As our model in Chapter 5 suggests, these are the context elements surrounding the jobs people do. Frederick Herzberg's analogy to hygiene seems very appropriate. Such elements are very important to, though not necessarily sufficient for, high levels of motivation. Certainly an employee will turn off pretty quickly without them. Who can imagine anyone working without adequate pay, under poor working conditions, while ill-treated, with no recognition, and without knowing why he is doing what he is doing? At least one would not work under those conditions for very long.

At the same time, however, these context, or hygiene, factors are not enough for sustaining, much less building, real commitment to one's job. The motivation crisis in the auto industry illustrates this most graphically—pay is relatively high and is about the only thing that holds or attracts new people to it. But the current indications are that even high pay is losing its holding power; it certainly is not building commitment to the job. Consequently the situation is becoming critical. There has to be something else for building true job commitment and motivation.

As discussed in the model in Chapter 5, this critical "something else" is represented by content factors. The model suggests that there are three main thrusts needed to combat job decay, to wind up ability and motivation for people in today's industrial environment. These three elements must supplement the traditional good personnel practices outlined above; without them there will be no real job commitment. They are—

(a) Personal growth opportunities through the work itself,
(b) Demands the job makes on the individual, and
(c) Factors affecting his ability to get the job done.

The next three chapters describe approaches to enhance each of these factors. Providing these three inputs is within the range of present-day motivation technologies and is the key to winding up today's organization to combat the motivation crisis as it exists today. And undoubtedly new motivation technologies will be developed within the same framework to sustain ability and commitment tomorrow. The concluding chapter discusses possible shapes of the new technologies.

8

INDIVIDUAL DEVELOPMENT

THIS PARTICULAR PHASE of the motivation program is designed to insure that key employees find a real opportunity for personal advancement in their careers, that they work in an environment providing personal growth, and that they are helped rather than blocked by the organization in realizing their own potentials and achieving their most important personal goals. Our interest is in outlining the key considerations in preventing barriers in the job relationships that tend to stunt employee growth and lead to obsolescence and lack of motivation.

This phase of a forward-thinking motivation program cannot stand alone. It must be supplemented by two other components, which we shall discuss in the following two chapters: (1) programs of job development to insure that work is meaningful and challenging and (2) organization development to minimize factors within the work setting

Major parts of this chapter are adapted from J. R. Hinrichs, "Two Approaches to Filling the Management Gap: Management Selection vs. Management Development," Personnel Journal, December 1970, pp. 1008–1014. Used with permission.

that detract from employees' ability to do their jobs in a fashion that will provide them with maximum satisfaction and motivation.

In this chapter we shall place primary emphasis on the individual development of high-potential employees. This does not mean that an enlightened organization will be unconcerned with providing personal growth opportunities to other employees. It merely recognizes that the personnel resource with the greatest potential for future contribution will rightly receive first priority. If high potential remains hidden, if talent is allowed to wind down and become obsolete, or if the orderly development of key employees and executives is cut off because of high attrition, the life of the enterprise is in jeopardy.

The approaches outlined in this chapter apply to all personnel. As we proceed with our discussion it should become clear that one of our prime considerations is to uncover potential talent wherever it may be in the workforce. We shall spend some time discussing specific systematic techniques for doing so.

As time goes on, however, our techniques will begin to sort out the probable potential of individual employees. Our assessments will suggest that certain development efforts we may put into place will be more effective with high-potential employees than if applied broadly. Here our development effort begins to take on a specialized character. It becomes tailored to the needs and potentials of individual employees whom we anticipate will grow into the organization leaders of tomorrow.

There must be and still will be development activity beamed at the rank-and-file employees; technology moves too fast not to continually polish and upgrade the skills of all the workforce. We all need recognition and the feeling of competence. The opportunity for growth and recognition must always be available to every employee.

But our major concern and our orientation in this chapter will be on the identification and development of talent among high-potential employees. This means the identification and development of management and executive talent, although the talent and potential of a more specialized nature such as that of professional staff specialists can be considered within the same framework. In addition, our orientation will be on the early identification and development of managerial talent.

We stress *early* for several reasons. First, as our previous discussions outlined, the early career years of high-potential employees are critical in the winding down process, or, conversely, in the upward spiral of motivation. If personal growth and development is allowed to drift, it may be too late for high-potential individuals.

Second, we stress early identification and development because it's just plain needed. With an absolute decline in the 1960s and stability in the 1970s in the age bracket 35 to 44—the key source of managers—we must continue to identify and promote managerial talent relatively early in their careers.

Now let's consider how this can be done. Our first concern will be with personnel development. The basic question is: How can we identify individuals who possess a greater than chance probability of being successful in key positions? Then we shall turn to the second aspect of

the development process: What special attention and training will be useful in insuring that this potential flowers?
We shall also attempt to tie these two aspects together into
a coordinated program for the early identification of management potential.

The primary method of developing an adequate
supply of skilled manpower has been training. American
industry has spent millions, if not billions, of dollars on
management development, not to mention the vast sums
spent on skills training for operatives and technicians.
Over the past 25 years the literature on management development has been replete with discussions of leadership
training, job rotation, sensitivity training, on-the-job
coaching, results-oriented appraisals, and on and on and
on.

Recently, a somewhat different slant to the management resources question has been appearing more regularly. This is built around the selection model, and we are
hearing more and more of companies that are developing
programs and approaches for the early identification of
management potential among their employees. The philosophy is one of developing programs to tag high-potential
individuals early in their careers so that they may be properly motivated and adequately rewarded to remain with
the organization and so that they may be appropriately
groomed for management careers.

Today, so many companies are flocking toward the
early identification model that one begins to wonder
whether there's a bandwagon effect operating, as is true of
so many new personnel programs. And if not a band-

wagon, doesn't much of the concern with early identification border on blind acceptance of what amounts to a "youth cult"?

Undoubtedly, there are some good reasons for a company's concern with early identification of management potential, and we shall outline these shortly. But there are also some occasions when a company should not be concerned about it. Before jumping onto the bandwagon, a company should do some hard soul-searching to determine whether this is what makes the most sense in filling its management requirements.

Early identification probably is not the answer when—

A company has relatively limited requirements for managers, so that it is not too difficult to fill openings through natural progression;

The nature of the management job is not overly complex, so that high levels of skills are not required and special attention to high potential is not particularly called for; or

A company is able to hire all the managers it needs on the outside and finds that cheaper. "Cheaper" entails both the dollar expenses of management development or early identification programs, and the morale and commitment expenses on the part of present employees when a promotion-from-within policy is not followed.

There probably are other instances where a dispassionate analysis of the situation would suggest that an early identification program is superfluous. One suspects, however, that very few companies bother to go through a critical analysis.

On the other hand, there are very clearly some circumstances in which an organization would be well advised to develop an early identification program, and many organizations today are finding themselves in these situations. For example, an early identification program might be suggested for a company characterized by—

A high degree of organizational complexity, requiring general managers with systematic broad exposure to a spectrum of organizational functions and a deliberate period of seasoning of their executive skills;

Rapid growth, which implies a high quantitative demand for managers, not to mention qualitative demands;

Change—in technologies, markets, organization—which inevitably results in much managerial obsolescence;

Physical demands, which put a premium on youth and vigor; and

A high rate of turnover, which puts a special premium on programs to hold high-potential employees.

Clearly, many organizations today are characterized by one if not all of these attributes; certainly not all the current concern with the early identification of management potential results from a bandwagon effect or a "youth cult."

An Ideal Program for Early Identification

An ideal program for identifying and developing an adequate supply of management talent would focus on two basic objectives: (a) to build a program appropriate for developing management talent at all levels of organization, from first-line managers up through top executives, and (b) to superimpose on this a program to systematically assess management potential and to identify individuals with high potential for responsible executive positions.

The intention is to get those individuals into the channels for top jobs in the organization within, say, ten years of their date of hire. High-potential individuals will not necessarily be placed in key executive jobs within ten years, but they will have been clearly identified and included in a systematic program of executive resources review. Typically, this means that the pool from which future top executives will come will be firmly identified by approximately age 35.

CHARACTERISTICS OF AN EARLY
IDENTIFICATION PROGRAM

One of the most useful ways to think of an early identification program is as an adaptation of the classic selection model industrial psychologists have used since World War I. In a nutshell, the model consists of procedures designed to evaluate currently available information about individuals in order to make a judgment about their probable future behavior. There are three major components of the model:

What it is that you want to make predictions about—the "criteria" to be used in early identification programs. This means defining and measuring whatever it is that constitutes successful executive or management behavior.

What will be evaluated as a basis for making judgments about future behavior—the predictors.

Evaluation of correlation between the predictors and the criteria. That is, there must be some concern with the degree of accuracy (or validity) with which the predictors can measure the behavior characterized by the criteria.

These three components have formed the backbone of selection programs for the past 50 years; they must also form the backbone of an early identification program.

A general principle that has been applied in selection also applies in early identification: human behavior tends to repeat itself. This merely says that one of the best predictors of what a person will do in the future is what he or she has done in the past.

This general principle is also part of the basic groundwork for an early identification program. But there are some distinct features that call for a slightly different interpretation of the classic model. First, much of the prediction cannot be performance-based. We must make a relatively large leap from an evaluation of performance in nonmanagement jobs to a prediction of performance in management positions. We do this, of course, but to the extent possible we bring an array of other predictors into the process.

Second, in contrast to the classic selection model, the distinction between predictors and criteria is less clear-cut in the early identification process. Instead, it is more fruitful to think of a selection procedure that continues throughout the entire career progression. Predictors at one point in time may be related to criteria at another, and those criteria in turn become predictors relating to subsequent criterion measures, and so forth. Initially, for example, we may want to assess training performance in a pre-management training program as a criterion. Some of our early tests, interviews, and other measures may be designed primarily to predict that criterion. At a later point in the career development of managers, training performance in the pre-manager program may be fruitfully thought of as a predictor and used as an input to assess the probable future management potential of the individuals. So, in contrast to selection programs designed for initial hiring, through the course of the early identification process one piece of data may serve as both a criterion and a predictor.

A number of other important points must be kept in mind, and we shall review them before describing an ideal program.

1. As is true of any selection program, an early identification program is a probability process. This means that we can never be a hundred percent sure about any predictions. Sometimes we will be wrong. So, when all our predictors are evaluated and we conclude that an individual has high potential for management, we should express our opinion something like this: "The odds are two to one [or whatever the degree of precision our prediction scheme allows us to state] that this individual may be a high performer as a manager." But we should never lose sight of the fact that, conversely, the odds are one out of three that he will be something other than highly successful.

2. The second point ties in very closely with the first: the prediction process must not be seen as a means of irrevocably designating high potential. As additional information is gathered and evaluated throughout the total career development process, we should expect that some people who are on the preliminary high-potential list will move off, and new people will move on.

3. As we mentioned, the early identification program should be multifaceted, using many predictors and multiple criteria, rather than just one input or a limited number of inputs. We do the same thing in the normal hiring process, evaluating interviews, background information, and perhaps test information to make predictions about productivity, turnover, or absenteeism. The early identification program should adopt a similar strategy.

4. In such an important function as early identification of management potential, the prediction procedures and evaluations must be standardized and universally applied throughout the organization. A major concern should be to avoid overlooking good people with potential and insuring that all employees are evaluated against the same standards and have the same opportunity for selection into any specially designated pool of high-potential talent.

5. As with any selection procedure, an early identification program must be tailor-made to a specific organization. Because of the variability between organizations in mission, climate, structure, and manpower talent, it would be a serious mistake to think that a program developed to fill the needs of one organization can operate effectively in another.

6. Early identification procedures must be validated within the environment in which they are to be used. This implies some degree of research to be sure that predictors are in fact related to criteria, to highlight those elements of the prediction scheme that should be given the most weight, and to insure that the program is implemented under a set of standardized ground rules.

7. A distinctive aspect of an early identification program is the recognition that there has to be some overlap between the assessment procedure and the development process. Generally, educators say that this is bad. Their contention is that evaluation or assessment of potential tends to generate stress and anxiety on the part of the people who are being evaluated and that this is detrimental to learning or personnel development. Within limited situations this is probably true. A stressful, anxiety-ridden classroom is generally not conducive to learning. But in the management arena it is impossible to separate the two; in fact it is desirable to systematically tie them together. Both are ongoing parts of the career development process. The program should be shaped so that management development contributes to assessment, and assessment in turn contributes to development. Later we shall illustrate how the two approaches can be tied together.

8. Although we have stressed the importance of research to validate the prediction procedures, many key elements in the determination of management potential are not susceptible to statement in hard, quantitative terms or to manipulation as statistical concepts. Statistical prediction statements should be made where possible but must

be supplemented by informed judgment. The assessment process should look at all available indicators of management potential—quantitative as well as qualitative—and match them against both quantitative and qualitative evaluations of future job requirements to make a judgment of the probable potential of the individual.

9. Probably the key requirement for the success of an early identification program is that the final judgment should be made by responsible line managers, not by a staff group. Typically, the staff job in the program consists of assembling all available information about potential candidates. But there are severe potential pitfalls involved in letting staff assume responsibility for the final designation.

First, staff employees do not have the perspective about the requirements for managerial success that line managers have. And the perspective of line managers tends not to find its way into the judgmental decision process.

Second, the early identification process is viewed by line managers as just another staff exercise and thus is not ascribed the level of importance it must have to receive support throughout the organization.

Third, if line managers actually "own" the decisions that are made in the final designation, they are much more apt to use them than if they are able to sit back and protest: "NIH" (not invented here) when high-potential employees are considered for managerial succession.

10. Experience in a number of major companies has shown that the most critical factor in the success of an

early identification program is the extent to which top management is involved in and supports the whole executive resources program.

SPECIFIC ASSESSMENT TECHNIQUES

There are a number of tools, techniques, and data inputs that probably should be built into any program for assessing managerial potential.

1. *Paper and pencil tests.* These include ability, aptitude, personality, and interest tests as well as various biographical and background inventories. Many companies have found them to be very useful inputs at various points during the assessment procedure. Exxon Corporation has been a pioneer in the use of standardized tests and inventories for the early identification of management potential.

2. *Interviews.* Systematic interviews by both staff members and outside consultants might be used as assessment tools.

3. *Training grades and ratings.* Information on how individuals have done in the various formal training programs in which they have participated should be considered for use as part of the total assessment procedure.

4. *Performance evaluations.* Certainly some evaluations should come out of periodic performance appraisals, but other indicators of performance such as sales figures, attainment of financial or profit objectives, or salary growth may be valuable inputs to the assessment process. Also, special nominations through such techniques as outstanding employee lists or promotability lists may be useful.

5. *"Situational" testing.* Recently a number of compa-

nies have been using various kinds of games and exercises as part of their assessment procedures. These include business game situations in which performance is evaluated; for example, the in-basket exercise, which simulates the correspondence a manager may receive in a typical day and evaluates his reactions to it, and formal assessment centers where employees participate in a number of exercises such as leaderless group discussions or decision-making games and their performance is systematically evaluated.

6. *Peer evaluations.* These have been found to be very useful, particularly in some extensive research conducted by the military services, and should be considered for use as part of the total assessment procedure. One very appropriate approach is to collect peer evaluations as part of the situational tests conducted in an assessment center. Studies of the validity of peer evaluations collected in conjunction with executive development sessions in industry suggest that one's cohorts in training can make more valid predictions of probable success in executive jobs than the staff of the executive development center.

Management Development

The management development side of our ideal program covers a number of components. Most are not especially new, but our program would tie them together systematically.

1. *Formal training.* We would include both formal training within the company and formal programs at out-

side locations, such as universities and executive development centers.

2. *On-the-job development.* Attention to on-the-job coaching, job rotation programs, and special development assignments would be a key part of our program.

3. *Performance appraisals.* We would use the development aspects of the appraisal process, including the performance review feedback sessions and the process of management by objectives and mutual goal setting, which are increasingly being used in industry.

4. *Individual development planning.* Our ideal management development program would include here the traditional replacement tables, which are among the stock and trade of management development departments. Such tables list the key positions of the organization, identify the incumbents in those positions, and list one or two individuals who would be likely candidates if the incumbent were to be promoted out, transferred, or leave. We would also use a systematic executive resources review, a program in which key line managers are brought into the decision-making process in evaluating management potential and in mapping the development plans for high-potential employees.

5. *Recognition programs.* These are designed to sustain the motivation of high-potential employees, by recognizing their contributions and by building motivation for self-development and growth. The programs would provide such things as awards for outstanding performance, publicity, and certainly accelerated compensation plans including, where feasible, stock options at a relatively early point in the high-potential employee's career.

All this sounds fine in broad outline. However, several recent reviews of the effectiveness of personnel training in general, and management development training in particular, present a rather bleak scene. Since formal management development training is the major component of the development side of our ideal program, it may be useful to review some of the problems.

1. The field is dominated by practitioners, most of whom are not professionally trained educators, psychologists, or learning specialists.

2. The emphasis tends to be on doing something, anything that seems to respond to organizational needs. In the rush to "do something," the practitioners all too often lose sight of the real problem. For example, having pinned down the fact that an organization will spend money and time to develop its management population, a typical reaction of the training department is to jump in with a fixed "program." Characteristic responses are: "Let's brush up that same program we gave last year." "ABC company is doing XYZ, we should too." "Obviously our managers need to know some of x, some of y, and a little of z. We'll put together a training smorgasbord that covers the waterfront."

Only rarely is time spent in determining in detail just what the training should accomplish. Usually there is only a very imprecise idea of the specific leadership tasks managers should be trained for. Very seldom is there any understanding of the basic components that make up the task. Finally, there usually is no determination of how to achieve proficiency in each component task, or how to link tasks together to achieve proficiency in the total task. In effect, there is seldom a rational analysis of how the training program should be constructed, much less any carefully controlled research to evaluate the process.

A voluminous catalog of training programs undoubtedly gives the illusion that problems are being solved as well as provides a measure of job security for the program implementer and administrator. But it does little to move management development beyond the seat of the pants approach that has characterized it for the past few decades.

3. With the premium on generating programs and relatively less concern with defining problems, program design becomes eclectic. Fads move in and out of use with the greatest of ease.

4. Today there is little or no concern with using basic theory about learning and personnel development in the design of programs, much less with building new theory. The "good" program is one that is attention-getting, dramatic, contemporary, or fun. Whether or not it changes behavior becomes secondary. And whether or not insights evolve for modifying the program to maximize results or for building new programs is of little concern.

5. Within this framework, of course, there is precious little research on the effectiveness of training. Most programs are sold and accepted on faith.

6. The whole situation is little different from what it was back in the 1950s or even the 1940s. While the content and emphasis of management development might have changed, the way in which training in most organizations is designed and implemented has evolved very little.

Against this rather disorganized backdrop, one might

question why training has survived at all as a viable organizational activity. And survive it has! Estimates of man-hours expended and dollars devoted to training and management development each year in American industry boggle the mind. The trend is not toward less reliance on training but toward more. While the practitioners are doing little to build a body of basic knowledge about the training and development process, they must be doing something right; it can't all be a big fraud.

Undoubtedly many things are being done right, or at least well. In all probability management development and training often do contribute to both individual and organizational effectiveness. A body of expertise and lore regarding what seems to work and what not to work has evolved.

But we contend that management development could be done better. We point out that it is as important to understand *why* certain things work as it is to identify *which* ones work so that insights may be generalized and applied to new areas. We suggest that to achieve this the technology of training should be built less on ad hoc considerations and more on general principles derived from systematic research and analysis. The alternative is for a review of the field of management development in the 1980s to read much the same as a review in the 1970s.

Part of the concern of a coordinated program for early identification and development of management is to encourage a more systematic analysis of development needs, to provide continuing feedback on the effectiveness of the development effort, and to provide the optimal sequencing of development activity to enhance managerial skills early in the individual's career. It is a step in the direction of a more systematic program with the ability to tailor training and other developmental activities to individual needs, to learn from results achieved or not achieved, and to provide correction and modification as necessary. It is a step beyond the disorganized ad hoc approaches characteristic of traditional management development programs. The key is the process of systematically tying the assessment and development activities together in the early (first 15 years or so) career progression.

MERGING MANAGEMENT ASSESSMENT AND MANAGEMENT DEVELOPMENT

Figure 7 outlines how the different components of the management development process might be brought into play at various points during the career progression of high-potential employees. We have concentrated on the critical first 15 years. The figure suggests that formal training might be used throughout this period, consisting of some form of initial skills training, some pre-management training perhaps after four years with the company, a first management development course at the point of promotion into first-line management, perhaps some outside program after ten years, and subsequently executive development, either in the company or at an outside center, for those who end up on the high-potential roster.

Performance appraisal and review is a regular part of the management development process, continuing throughout the total time period, and may take the form of results-oriented evaluation and goal setting after the first

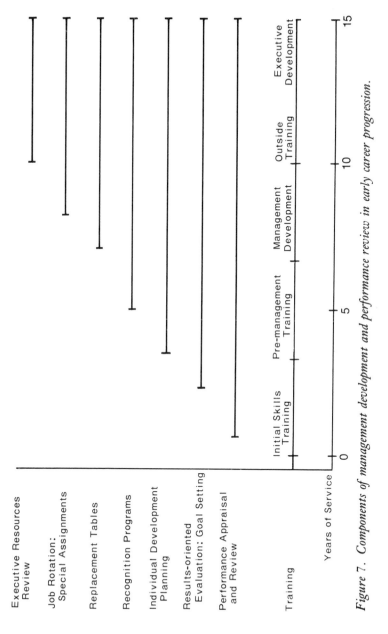

Figure 7. Components of management development and performance review in early career progression.

few years. Individual development plans probably come into play when the high-potential individual is eligible for promotion to first-line management, and recognition programs about the same time. The high-potential employee might begin to show up on systematic replacement tables after five years in the company, and job rotation and special assignments might begin to be planned for him at the same point. If the program functions correctly, after ten years of service the high-potential employee should be included in the systematic executive resources review.

The other side of the coin is the assessment process. Figure 8 illustrates how the various assessment tools and

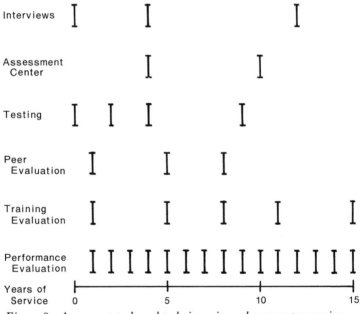

Figure 8. Assessment tools and techniques in early career progression.

techniques might be melded into the 15-year career development process. Performance evaluations and appraisals probably would be collected on a yearly basis. At each point at which the individual participated in a formal training program there might be some evaluation of his performance in the training situation that could be brought into the total assessment picture. Peer evaluations might also flow out of the training situation, particularly initial skills training, pre-management training, and first-line management training. This type of evaluation could consist of either general ratings of the individual's performance by his peers or some kind of sociometric nomination in which participants in the training are asked to select one or two individuals (or rank the capabilities of the total group) as chief executive in a hypothetical business undertaking. Perhaps various training classes might be asked to elect a class president and a vice-president on the basis of overall contribution.

Formal paper and pencil tests might occur at a number of points in career progression, including the initial selection point, with a more comprehensive battery of tests after several years, and another battery in conjunction with a formal assessment center using situational tests. Perhaps there might be a final battery of tests later in the career, focusing primarily on such areas as management judgment and systematically evaluating background information keyed to the early employment period. Several companies have used this sequential approach to psychological testing.

A formal assessment center might be used at several

points. The first might be before promotion to first-line management, where it probably can make its biggest contribution by providing information about probable performance in management through simulating many aspects of the management job. Another assessment center might be used before promotion into executive positions and might employ slightly different techniques and procedures.

Formal interviews might enter the assessment procedure at several points, once as part of initial hiring, again in conjunction with a formal assessment center, and perhaps later in the career as part of the executive resources review. Either staff members or outside psychologists might conduct the interviews.

When Figures 7 and 8 are compared, it is clear that the management development process is an ongoing activity that can be overlaid with a number of factors designed to contribute to the management assessment process. This ideal program should fill the basic objectives set for it: (a) systematically providing candidates for all levels of management and (b) identifying early in their careers those with the potential for high-level management positions. It should also be clear that these two functions have to be tied together and coordinated, that each contributes to the other, and that both management assessment and management development are cumulative processes occurring throughout the early career span of high-potential employees. With this in mind, it should be possible to build a comprehensive program for the early identification of management potential and to tailor it to a specific organization with some assurance that the management skills so much in demand are available when needed. By insuring that key employees are systematically moved through careers that fully use their skills and abilities and enhance their sense of personal growth, an organization will take an important step toward warding off the winding down process.

9
JOB
DEVELOPMENT

PROBABLY ONE OF the most widely discussed management strategies in recent years is job enrichment. Judging from the number of articles, books, and conferences dealing with job enrichment theory and practice, it seems that this emerging technology has become the newest management fad, following in the footsteps of such well-known activities as T-groups, management by objectives (MBO), Grid® training, and participative management.

Job enrichment is not necessarily a new concept. It dates back to the 1940s, when in the form of job enlargement it was systematically implemented and evaluated in the manufacturing environment of IBM.[1] Also, there is a qualitative difference between the concern over job enrichment and previous faddish interest in T-groups, grid training, and MBO. What has happened is that a theoretical base for job enrichment has been developed. Now it is easy to see how restructuring jobs can consistently fit into a framework of enhanced work motivation. In addition, there has been a great deal of interlocking research dramatically demonstrating that job enrichment can have a significant impact on productivity and job satisfaction in a wide range of work situations. Plus, perhaps most important, with the winding down process in industry reaching crisis proportions, the need for something like job enrichment has become so extreme that it has received great acceptance. It seems that job enrichment is a concept and a methodology whose time has arrived. In this chapter we shall explore both the concept and the methodology and attempt to show how job enrichment can be used as an antidote to the winding down process.

Job enrichment is clearly a powerful technology. One can quibble about where, when, and how to implement it, but there will be little doubt that it works. Although we do need to know more of the answers to the where, when, and how questions, we shall certainly consider it an important tool in enhancing job and company commitment and in building the perceived component of job demands discussed in Chapter 5.

What Is Job Development?

There is no clear, widely accepted definition of just what job development or job enrichment is. For example, *Fortune* comments:

> Job enrichment is a diffuse, open-ended kind of concept which is more an attitude or strategy than it is a definable entity. In fact there is no one term for it that is accepted by all the experts. But there are certain elements that appear characteristically wherever job enrichment is going on. Central, of course, is the basic idea of giving the

worker more of a say about what he or she is doing, including more responsibility for setting goals, and more responsibility for the excellence of the completed product. It can also mean, in appropriate kinds of plants, allowing the worker to carry assembly through several stages, sometimes even to completion and preliminary testing, rather than doing just one small operation endlessly.[2]

That discussion deals specifically with the concept of job enrichment. Job enrichment efforts focus on two major aspects of the working relationship: the content of work and the discretion people have to make decisions and provide variety in the way the work is performed.

In discussing the question of designing jobs to counteract the winding down process, however, we have chosen to use the broad concept of job development rather than the narrower framework of job enrichment. The process of *developing* jobs is a more inclusive one and seems more in keeping with our total area of concern. The theory and technology of job development rest on a number of key assumptions:

1. Sizable numbers of people are working in jobs that do not fully utilize their skills.
2. People are not inherently lazy; they need to have their skills more fully utilized in their work;
3. Given an opportunity, people will put more effort into their work;
4. When this occurs, their level of productivity will increase, as well as the satisfaction they derive from their work.

A recent report outlines several strands to the job development process, but they are somewhat diffuse and there is much overlap.[3]

Job rotation. An employee moves between different jobs to expand his knowledge and to build variety and increased skills acquisition into his job assignment. The individual tasks themselves are not changed, but the personal growth from learning different tasks and the relief from the boredom of doing a single task will lead to enhanced work content.

Job enlargement. The job is expanded from a single central task to include other related tasks. When several tasks are combined, variety is built into the job and the "cycle time," or time from starting task one to completing task ten, is increased. The added tasks are not necessarily more demanding of the employee, merely different. Job enlargement entails what has been characterized as "horizontal loading"—the coupling together of several tasks of roughly equal levels of difficulty.

Job enrichment. The main component that differentiates job enrichment from job enlargement is the concept of "vertical loading." Here the effort is to give the employee more of the whole job to do, usually delegating to him some functions generally thought of as managerial responsibilities. Necessarily, vertical loading adds elements to the job that entail more responsibility and decision making, more individual control over the work, and more discretion in the way it is carried out. The intention is to make the worker more responsible for a total job cycle, from planning and organizing, to doing the job, to evaluating and assessing results. In contrast to horizontal loading, which can be thought of as more of the same, vertical loading upgrades the nature of the work. In enriching the job, the traditional motivators from Frederick Herzberg's motivator-hygiene theory are emphasized: recognition, responsibility, personal growth, and intrinsically interesting work.

Plan, do, control. This is an extension of the job enrichment concept specifically developed at Texas Instruments by M. Scott Myers. The concept says that the worker must have considerable responsibility for the planning of what he will do, the doing, and the control aspect, which includes measurement and evaluation of the work and correction of problems. In other words, every worker must be viewed as the manager of the work he does, with concomitant managerial responsibilities. The concept also addresses the importance of many of the so-called hygiene items Herzberg very specifically ruled out of the job enrichment process. These include questions of participation in decision making, relationships with other people, pay, supervision, and working conditions.

Work simplification. This concept is probably the oldest form of job design and has its roots in the school of scientific management. The objective of work simplification is to examine in minute detail the actual processes by which a task is carried out and to make the task more efficient by eliminating unnecessary steps and combining steps wherever possible. When employees are involved in the job analysis and work simplification process, there can be positive motivational effects. In theory, however, work simplification tends to reduce the size of jobs, whereas job enlargement and job enrichment have the objective of increasing the content of jobs. But, when used to remove unnecessary aspects of jobs, the work simplification approach can be a valuable part of job development.

In the concept of job development we include all the approaches and methodologies designed to alter the content of jobs so as to enhance employees' motivational potential. Job development consists of whatever can be done to design jobs so that they are more rewarding, and thus less susceptible to the winding down process.

JOB DEVELOPMENT PROGRAMS

One of the striking aspects of the current scene in American business is the extent to which job design has taken hold as a formal program in many organizations. It has begun to obtain the stature of such tried-and-true programs as salary administration, management development, and job evaluation. Although there is a certain amount of cant and faddism in the job development process, and it remains to be seen if the emphasis on it will last, we believe it will.

Robert Ford writes about AT&T, one of the pioneers in the job development movement:

> Quite clearly AT&T is settling down for the long haul. Seventy-seven new programs have been started. No one expects all jobs to be equally improvable, nor is every job in need of assistance. And, since there are so many requests, the accepted view is, don't push any manager who is uncertain or lukewarm in his interest. Reach him later.

At this writing [1969] more than 50 companies outside the Bell System have requested further information about the studies; others have now started here in the United States or abroad. A reasonably safe prediction is that much more information will be available within the next ten years as to how one bridges the gap from theory to fact.[4]

There are a number of reasons why we may logically expect job development programs to be broadly applied and to persist as a recognized component of effective management in the years to come.

The concept of job development is directly based on several of the most widely accepted theories of work motivation known today. For example, it clearly fits in with the concept of human needs we outlined earlier. In most contemporary organizations, the more basic needs—physiological needs, safety needs, and social needs—are pretty well satisfied. These are the things that dominated labor–management relations during the first half of this century. In the 1970s, relatively decent levels of pay, security, and respect for human dignity tend to be taken for granted.

The theory of human needs contends, however, that as basic needs are satisfied, behavior becomes motivated by other attributes. So it is a natural assumption that workers today are more and more concerned with self-esteem and an opportunity to realize their own potentials. The concepts and techniques employed in job development are specifically intended to build the potential for satisfying these needs into the daily work relationship.

Similarly, the theoretical position developed by

Douglas McGregor about work motivation is a very important underpinning of the job development process. McGregor contended over a decade ago that the traditional assumptions management had about employee motivation were outmoded.[5] These assumptions, which he called theory X, characterized the average employee as being lazy, a follower, not a leader, resistant to change, not too bright, indifferent to organizational needs.

McGregor's main thesis was that these assumptions were fallacious. When he formulated his own theory, behavioral science research was suggesting that an alternate set of assumptions about human motivation had greater validity, at least in the modern industrial scene. McGregor labeled these alternate assumptions theory Y. They maintained that—

1. People are *not* by nature passive or resistant to organizational needs. They have become so as a result of experience in organizations.

2. The motivation, the potential for development, the capacity for assuming responsibility, the readiness to direct behavior toward organizational goals are present in people. Management does not put them there. It is management's responsibility to make it possible for people to recognize and develop these characteristics for themselves.

3. The essential task of management is to arrange organizational conditions and methods of operation so that people can achieve their own goals best by directing their own efforts toward organizational objectives.

Very clearly, job development concepts that attempt to enhance work content and the amount of discretion employees have in how they do their work are built on theory Y assumptions rather than on theory X.

The final underpinning to job development in modern motivation theory comes from Frederick Herzberg.[6] The links here are even more directly visible than those of need satisfaction theory or of theory Y. Herzberg's theory flows from initial research done in 1959 that identified qualitative differences in the factors that led to job satisfaction as opposed to factors that led to job dissatisfaction for a group of professional employees (engineers and accountants). Subsequent research has refined the theory to the point where it is well known by anybody with even a brushing acquaintance with contemporary behavioral sciences. Herzberg's formulation says that one set of factors, if absent from the work environment, can cause dissatisfaction among employees. He initially termed such factors hygiene, but they have also been labeled maintenance factors, dissatisfiers or, as we have done in Chapter 5, job context items. These job elements, which include such things as company policy and administration, working conditions, interpersonal relations, quality of supervision, and pay, are important for preventing job dissatisfaction. When there are problems in these areas, employees will be dissatisfied, and it will be impossible for them to be highly motivated. Such hygiene elements can be thought of as a platform that must be built solidly in any healthy organization as a base for motivation.

But in and of themselves, these context elements are motivationally neutral. Without adequate hygiene, the organization is in trouble; with adequate hygiene, the organization may or may not have a motivated workforce. The issue of motivation depends on another set of factors: the satisfiers, motivators, or job content items. These items include achievement, recognition, advancement, responsibility, and the intrinsic challenge or interest the work itself offers.

Early attention in the job enrichment movement very consciously and deliberately—in many instances with the direct personal involvement of Professor Herzberg—made an effort to increase the number of motivators that can be associated with jobs. The dedication of Robert Ford's book describing research at AT&T is as concise a statement of the extent to which Herzberg's theoretical position underlies the job enrichment movement as any that could be stated: "To Professor Frederick Herzberg, humanist and psychologist, Case Western Reserve University, who stimulated our search for a way to introduce motivators into the work itself." [7]

The future of job development is probably relatively secure because it is eminently practical. There has been a conscious effort on the part of the pioneers in the field to prevent job development from being, or being seen as, another happiness program. The objectives are keyed to enhance job performance. It is emphasized that there will be no sacrifice of productivity to achieve worker satisfaction. In fact, the first and foremost concern is productivity. Almost all the research has concentrated primarily on productivity. Where implications of job development for job satisfaction have been evaluated, the assessment has very deliberately been secondary to evaluation in terms of performance. Thus job development is able to demonstrate that it is a worthwhile investment that yields a tangible return to organizations—increased performance, which is translated into increased profits.

Pioneers in job development have also made a conscious effort to keep the approach flexible and eclectic. An effort has been made to have a minimum of do's and don'ts. It was emphasized that there are many many ways of achieving the objectives of building motivators into jobs and that different approaches should be tried, depending on the particular organization or job under consideration. Although a certain amount of technique is becoming reified into job enrichment as more and more organizations move into the field, there probably is a good deal less of it than in such long-established personnel techniques as salary administration, hiring, or training. To the extent that the methodology remains flexible, its vitality most likely will be enhanced.

One of the biggest positive attributes of job development is that it is relatively simple. It is not necessary for someone with a lot of advanced training or knowledge of the behavioral sciences to serve as a job development coordinator. As a matter of fact, it probably is preferable if the coordinator is someone intimately involved in the day-to-day operation of the organization rather than a staff specialist. The concepts of job development make sense, even to the layman. And the implementation of job development concepts is relatively easy. In these conditions, there is a good potential for job development approaches to become an integral part of the management technology of an organization.

Probably one of the main reasons for expecting job development to continue in vogue is that it clearly fulfills a big need in organizations today. It is, without doubt, the most powerful direct technique available for combating the motivation crisis. As long as the crisis exists—and most likely it will persist for a long time—the methodology will be used.

Above all, we can expect job development to be used because it works. In study after study, in an extremely broad spectrum of work and organizational settings, it has been demonstrated that the methodology of job development can increase productivity. It is also clear that it often has powerful positive implications for job satisfaction. For the pragmatic American manager, when a methodology clearly helps him attain his organizational objectives, he will use it. If he does not, his competitors will use it and surely pass him by.

Cases

A few case histories of job development programs at work should help illustrate the results achieved in some areas in which the methodology has been applied. This is not an exhaustive list of experiences—the field is growing too fast for that—but is intended merely to give some idea of what has been done.

AMERICAN TELEPHONE AND TELEGRAPH

Probably the best-known program of job development exists at AT&T. The original draft of the report on that effort is included in the widely read book by Robert Ford:

Motivation Through the Work Itself,[8] and also is the subject of a motion picture produced by AT&T illustrating job development concepts.

The study was carried out in the stockholder relations section of the treasury department of AT&T. The study group consisted of 104 women who answered complaint letters from stockholders. Before the test, this particular group had been plagued by high turnover, very obvious strong job dissatisfaction, and a relatively poor showing for the department in terms of customer service.

The stockholder relations clerk's job was relatively narrow. Each clerk was given a specialized area of concern and answered only letters pertaining to that specific area, such as dividends. Standard form letters were used and were signed by the department manager.

When the job development test was implemented, some dramatic changes were made in the nature of the work. Each girl was permitted to handle correspondence pertaining to all aspects of stockholder relations. The form letters were eliminated and the girls drafted their own replies. These letters went out over their signature, and the responsibility for verifying the replies was delegated to the person handling the letter rather than being subjected to a quality control check by the manager.

When the test was evaluated after five months, the customer service index for the department had increased dramatically. In addition, the level of job satisfaction among the stockholder relations clerks had also increased significantly. Other positive benefits of the test were identified, such as tangible savings from eliminating the verification of replies, reduced turnover, reduced frequency of long absences, and increased promotion rates (presumably because of enhanced job performance by members of the test group). The overall reactions of both management and the people involved in the test were highly favorable. When the results were evaluated against those of control groups doing similar work without changes in job design, the conclusion pointed clearly to significant positive effects directly attributable to the job development program.

Another follow-up in the treasury department at AT&T after 18 months, although not carefully controlled against other departments where jobs were not enriched, suggested that very large dollar savings had been realized by the changes and probably would continue. Based primarily on reduced turnover and reductions in the number of personnel required in the department, an estimated total of directly attributable dollar saving of $558,000 was identified. Additional savings from increased productivity, improved customer service, and enhanced job satisfaction were not priced and not included in this estimate.

AT&T embarked on a number of additional trials or experiments based on this first study. In 1969, Robert Ford reported in his book that 77 new programs had been started and that AT&T was firmly convinced of the value and real return from these efforts.[9] Ford described 18 of the studies at AT&T, in addition to the original study in its treasury department. The studies covered a wide range of employees, including toll operators, keypunch operators, framemen, installers, and service representatives. In almost all cases, both performance and attitudes were very positively affected by the job development efforts.

TEXAS INSTRUMENTS

Job development has been applied to a number of jobs at Texas Instruments. The concept of plan, do, control has evolved from this work. The concept is explained fully in M. Scott Myers' book *Every Employee a Manager*.[10] Basically, under this approach each employee is given as much responsibility as possible for planning his own work, for doing it, and for controlling it through measurement, evaluation, and correction.

One of the more interesting applications of job development at Texas Instruments was with janitorial personnel. The results of this project suggest considerable potential for the job enrichment model, even at unskilled and menial jobs that many have felt are incapable of being enriched.[11]

The project was initiated as a result of dissatisfaction with the quality of cleaning service provided by a contractor at TI's Dallas headquarters. The decision was made to test the feasibility of having TI employees perform the cleaning services, while simultaneously trying to develop the job through the concept of plan, do, control. Some of the steps taken were:

1. Teams of matrons and male attendants were formed and encouraged to exercise initiative in identifying and solving problems.
2. Training and new equipment were provided.
3. The employees were given broad job responsibilities, but the details for carrying them out were left to their own initiative.

4. The employees developed their own work schedules and procedures to meet their objectives.
5. They were also given responsibility for measuring their own performance.
6. Overall, supervision attempted to operate under the basic assumptions of theory Y, with expectations that even for relatively menial jobs, workers are motivated and want to do well as long as the job situation allows them to do so.

Although no control groups were evaluated against this group, changes following the implementation of the job development factors were impressive.

1. Ratings of the cleanliness level rose from 65 to 85 percent.
2. Turnover during each quarter of the year dropped from 100 percent when the contractor was doing the cleaning to 9.8 percent when TI personnel were assigned the job.
3. The number of people required to do the cleaning dropped from 120 to 70.
4. Management approved the extension of the concept to the entire site.
5. Annual savings of $103,000 for the entire site were registered; this figure was based on the differences between contractor fees and the cost of labor, materials, and overhead when the service was performed by TI employees.
6. The reactions of the employees themselves were extremely positive.

Because of its extensive, very positive experiences with its own tailor-made approach to job development, Texas Instruments continues to use the concept as an integral part of its operating procedures.

IMPERIAL CHEMICAL INDUSTRIES, LTD.

A number of studies have been carried out in the United Kingdom showing the applicability of job development methods to a variety of work, both at ICI and other British companies. Results of these studies are described in a *Harvard Business Review* article.[12] The studies covered such diverse groups as:

Laboratory technicians. The technicians were encouraged to write many of the final reports on research projects, were more involved in planning projects and setting targets, were given more opportunity to follow up on their own ideas, were authorized to requisition materials and equipment and order services, and were more involved in training and interviewing job applicants. Systematic follow-up on the write-ups of research projects showed remarkable improvements in the quality of monthly reports under the developed job. The quality level almost equaled that of the reports submitted by the scientists.

Sales representatives. Salesmen were given considerable new authority to plan and manage their territories, discretionary range in setting the prices of products, some authority to make immediate monetary settlements against customer complaints, and considerable latitude in handling customer complaints about faulty materials. The results suggested a significant increase in sale and volume, compared with a control group in which these changes were not made.

Design engineers. Experienced engineers were given complete independence in running their projects, including greater authority over spending money, selecting and placing support personnel, and authorizing overtime. The major impact was a significant increase in the level of job satisfaction in the test group. In addition, the overall evaluation of the new procedures by senior management was quite positive.

Factory supervisors. The results of two experiments to substantially increase the planning and financial responsibility as well as managerial authority of foremen were also evaluated as being quite positive.

The studies at ICI and other British corporations are particularly impressive because they illustrate the range of positions for which job development efforts may be appropriate. They also document many of the specific changes that were made to enhance those jobs and that can be implemented in similar jobs in other settings.

INTERNATIONAL BUSINESS MACHINES CORPORATION
Job development has had a long history at IBM; one of the first instances of an effort to systematically enlarge a job took place in 1943 at the Endicott, New York, plant. Senior management noticed the human and organizational inefficiency entailed in having a milling machine operator stand by idly waiting for the set-up man to adjust the machine and an inspector to test the adjustment. Management decided to give the operator all those responsibilities.

The experience under the enlarged job was extremely positive, in terms of both job performance and job statisfaction.

More recently, IBM has implemented a great many job development projects. Most of them are in manufacturing jobs, including such positions as machine operator, inspector, assembler, laboratory specialist, and operations involved in manufacturing semiconductors. Many of these projects have been systematically evaluated, and impressive effects in terms of productivity and job satisfaction have become commonplace.[13] The concept of job development, first introduced in IBM in the 1940s, has grown significantly into a broad-based company program, both in the United States and overseas.

GENERAL FOODS

Another of the more interesting examples of job enrichment at work is in an experiment undertaken by General Foods at its pet food processing plant at Topeka, Kansas.[14] The new plant, opened in 1971, has been used as a laboratory to check out some of the job development concepts of worker motivation. The production tasks were assigned to teams of 7 to 17 members, and each worker learned all the jobs required of the team. In place of conventional department heads, team leaders were assigned. The teams are responsible for correcting customer complaints, deciding when their teammates have mastered all operations of the job and are qualified to receive the team pay rate, and many of the day-to-day decisions about performing the work.

General Foods has found the program to be highly

successful. First, the plant was opened with about 90 employees, or 25 percent fewer than ordinarily would have been needed. Absenteeism is running about one percent, which is significantly below that of comparable industries. Turnover has been quite low. The productivity of the plant has been running about 40 percent higher per manday than in comparable General Foods plants.

General Foods is currently planning to install many of the procedures developed in the test at Topeka in other areas of its operations. Job design is rapidly becoming a way of life.

VOLVO AND SAAB

These two companies have taken the bull by the horns in tackling the blue collar blues rampant in the automobile industry.[15] Rather than professing impotence to do anything about the supposedly inexorable demands of the auto assembly line, the two manufacturers have drawn on job development concepts to redesign the entire assembly process. It is a daring—and costly—experiment, and not all the results are in. But the indications are that Volvo and Saab may be onto some important new methodologies for revitalizing an industry that many feel is beyond hope.

The experiment at the Saab plant involves 30 of some 300 employees in an engine manufacturing plant. The test employees are organized into three-person teams. Instead of each employee performing a repetitive operation on an assembly line, the entire engine is moved into a workshop where the team works together to complete the final assembly—adding carburetor, spark plugs, water pump, and so on. The operation takes 30 minutes, and the team members decide how they will allocate the specific tasks. New engines to be completed are brought in only when the team calls for them rather than being fed to them on a paced assembly line.

Initial evaluation shows that productivity for the test group is roughly the same as it was on the traditional assembly line but that absenteeism and turnover, which had been serious problems, have been significantly reduced. The costs are primarily in greater training time and investment, as well as in plant space, but the preliminary assessment is that the costs are worth the reduction in absenteeism and turnover.

At Volvo, production methods have been changed to permit a team of workers to follow a bus chassis down the production line, performing a number of operations over a period of 90 minutes.

Thus the workers have a great deal more variety in their work, more of a sense of completion, and more identity with the job. While considerable training is involved in getting people to be proficient in all the different tasks, preliminary evaluations show that the results are basically positive. A quality control index seems to have improved significantly, and turnover has declined.

Volvo's enthusiasm for implementing job development concepts is probably best expressed by the $21 million it is investing in a new assembly plant. The work process is being organized around teams, and the long assembly line has been broken down into five sections in a unique factory that will be built in the form of a five-pointed star. Although Volvo says that the cost of the factory is greater than it would have been under a more conventional design, it anticipates that production will be at least comparable, and many of the demeaning aspects of the assembly process will be reduced.

Many, many other examples of specific attempts at job development could be cited, along with impressive information on the results achieved. For example, the Conference Board reports in some detail case studies from Arapahoe Chemicals, the Internal Revenue Service, Weyerhaeuser Company, the Valley National Bank, Pittsburg Plate Glass Industries, and Monsanto.[16] *Business Week* discusses job development efforts at TRW Systems, General Electric, and others.[17] *Fortune* cites information from the R. G. Barry Corporation in Columbus, Ohio, Corning Glass, Donnelly Mirrors, Polaroid, Non-Linear Systems, Precision Cast Parts, and others.[18] At Western Union job enrichment efforts have been systematically linked to organization development with evidently impressive results.[19]

This brief list of examples could be extended almost indefinitely. The only conclusions one can make are:

1. The concept has received broad management support in both the United States and abroad.
2. It has been applied to a variety of work and organizations.
3. Many different approaches to job development are possible.
4. Almost without exception the results seem to be positive.

There can be little doubt that job development is one of the more powerful methodologies available today for combating the winding down process.

As the preceding cases illustrate, there has been a considerable amount of experience in a number of organizations in the actual implementation of job development. Out of this have grown many insights that practitioners in the field use more or less regularly. Although participants in the job development movement emphasize that the approach should be flexible and eclectic, at the same time experience has proved specific approaches and concepts to be very useful. The remainder of this chapter will review some of these to provide a framework for job development implementation. First, it would be useful to review some of the obstacles an organization inevitably will face when it begins to move into this new area.

Typical Obstacles to Job Development

Implementing job development, if done wholeheartedly rather than in a token manner, implies fundamental changes in many of the things organizations do and how they do them. The traditional approach to jobs has been to specialize and narrow them to the point where the required tasks are clearly identifiable and rationalized. Then measurements and controls have been implemented so that incumbents' performance in the task can be clearly and unambiguously assessed. All planning, decision-making, and evaluation responsibility is placed in the hands of management rather than the worker. Essentially workers are viewed as an extension of machines that perform routinized functions.

The job development concept implies moving away from traditional approaches. The fundamental change is to provide the worker himself with many managerial responsibilities, to make jobs richer and broader, rather than specialized, and to provide the worker with more autonomy in carrying out his assignments.

As such a concept begins to take hold we can expect several possibly unanticipated consequences for managers in the organization.[20] First, when workers have a taste of real responsibility, begin to realize that it is possible to attain a feeling of achievement and personal growth through their work, they will be reluctant to settle for less. But the job development process requires continual renewal. A job that is developed to provide challenge and achievement will not stay that way forever; once the job is mastered it will begin to decay unless additional attention is paid to further development. The worker, having realized the potential of engaging in meaningful, challenging work, will push out for more responsibility and further job development. As he does so, he may present problems to the manager. He will demand more. He will insist that the organization take positive steps to provide him more work that is satisfying and self-fulfilling.

Second, he will tend to become an iconoclast. As he realizes his potential more through the work, he will become more and more involved in the organization and will increasingly question things that stand in the way of his own job challenge and self-growth. He will also become more of a confronter. He will be more willing to engage in open dialog with management about work conditions. Thus one probable consequence of real job development is the creation and encouragement of a more vocal workforce, actively concerned about their role in the organization and willing to confront management over whatever seems to detract from their job satisfaction and motivation.

A fundamental question is whether management is ready, willing, or able to handle the confrontation. Or will many managers typically follow management by ostrich techniques? It is reasonable to assume, however, that if management is not ready to handle the consequences of job development, it will have the confrontation anyhow. The current motivation crisis in business suggests that this confrontation, if not here now, is certainly not far off. Job development appears to be a very necessary alternative to management by ostrich for any organization that hopes to weather this crisis.

On the basis of considerable experience with practical applications of job development, a list of 11 basic factors that inhibit the implementation of job development has been identified.[21] Recognition of these obstacles and a systematic plan for overcoming them are important to an organization that hopes to get a job development program moving. The obstacles are in the following areas.

Education. There is little possibility of getting anything started by merely including a discussion of job development in management development programs. Awareness of the theory and technique does not mean that managers know how to go about implementing job development.

Ideology. Despite the research and theory that support

the concept of job development, the old-fashioned beliefs about effective management in terms of measurement and control systems, specialization, and so forth are still widely entrenched in American managers. There is a strong possibility that very often job development will be seen as another "softheaded management" happiness program.

Organization. Organizational facts of life obstruct job development because it is often viewed as impinging on the perceived vested interests of various functions. There is also the problem of getting management to take a long-term view of improving jobs rather than concentrating on today's production, as well as the difficulty of maintaining organizational stability while job development efforts settle down.

Management. Job development can be threatening to managers and thus instinctively resisted. Change implies risk taking, and managers have a natural tendency to hold onto what is comfortable, tried, and familiar. There is also tacit admission that the way things were done before was not effective. Also, managers tend to feel that pushing responsibilities down to employees makes them lose control, waters down their own job, and is an admission that they themselves are redundant for many of the activities they have been doing.

Technology. Job development may involve considerable investment in changed facilities or technology. Managers frequently are just plain unwilling to make that investment.

The employee. Not all employees want or are capable of fulfilling enriched jobs. It is a mistake to assume that job development is a panacea; it needs to be tailored to the desires and abilities of individual employees.

The enricher. Often people who promote a concept like job development become overly evangelical in their approach. If they lose sight of the realities of the specific situation and begin to think in terms of universal applications and methodologies, their proposals will inevitably be seen as inappropriate or unrealistic.

Diagnosis. There must be systematic evaluation of the nature of an organization's problem to insure that job development is what is called for. In some organizations there are motivational problems, to be sure, but the jobs themselves are fully developed and highly challenging. An accurate diagnosis might suggest that the problem is in some other area; for example, in interpersonal relations or in bureaucratic constraints rather than in the nature of the work.

The prove-it-here reaction. Most managers tend to see their operation as unique and tend to question the suitability of a program or concept for their situation.

The nothing-new-here reaction. "So what's new, we've been doing it all along." Some people either do not see the unique aspects of job development or contend that they have always provided highly motivating jobs for their employees.

Time. A job development project does not just happen without the investment of considerable effort and time on the part of the management involved. Inevitably, managers will raise the objection that they just do not have the time to devote to this new program.

IMPLEMENTATION

There is no one best way to carry out a job development project. Some of the key components that should be considered in overcoming the obstacles to job enrichment are the following.

The decision of where, when, and how to implement job development should be based on a thorough diagnosis of organizational needs. The diagnosis entails systematic collection of information about factors affecting motivation and careful identification of whether in fact the problem involves job content. It can be done by looking at operating data, through interviews, or, as often is the case, by means of a detailed analysis of attitude and opinion survey information. Where survey results for a particular department point to widespread dissatisfaction with the degree to which skills are being used and the feeling that work is unchallenging and unsatisfying, this is a pretty good indicator that that particular department is ripe for a job development effort. The alternative to a systematic diagnosis is an attempt to blindly and on a broadside basis implement job development programs; the probability of success, however, is extremely doubtful.

After the problem areas have been identified, it is important to search for sympathetic management that is receptive to change. If the job development practitioner attempts to force his wares on line management, he will meet with resistance. In any organization it should be possible to find people sympathetic to new approaches. It is essential to have support from the line organization to successfully implement, not to mention sustain, a job development program.

Next, a demonstration test should be conducted. This aspect of the methodology is particularly important in organizations without prior experience with job development. Primarily on the basis of the experience at AT&T, it has become clear that the biggest boost in job development can come from a successful test in a specific organization. Then one can talk in concrete terms about what was done, how all obstacles were overcome, and what tangible results were achieved.

The resources for implementing job development must be provided. This means identifying key people who will have the responsibility for carrying out the project and for insuring that the effort is sustained. Then specific training in the theory and methodology of job development has to be given to these key people.

Typical training programs cover theories of work motivation and the theoretical basis for many of the design principles involved in job development. The key design principles of vertical loading, closure, and feedback are clarified. Some of the prime sources of building vertical loading into jobs are explored, including rearranging parts of the job, combining tasks, bringing in tasks ordinarily thought of as belonging to other functions, building new responsibility into the job, including functions traditionally performed by the manager, or eliminating from the job, through automation or delegation, tasks that do not require the skills and abilities of the incumbents.

The concept of closure emphasizes the importance of building a sense of completion and responsibility for a total job into the task. The training in concepts emphasizes the importance of building feedback into jobs. This provides the continuing possibility for people to have self-awareness of how they are doing and the opportunity to monitor, correct, and control the quality of their tasks.

Other typical aspects of training include a discussion of the methodology of implementing job development and of evaluating results. Often there can be practice and demonstrations in such aspects as brainstorming approaches to determine vertical loading for jobs, various exercises designed to increase group leadership skills of the key people, and training in techniques of selling management on job development concepts and promoting the program throughout the organization. In effect, the training should be designed to provide key people with the skills needed to implement and follow through on a job development program.

After training, the key person is then in a position to try to develop real-life jobs in his area of the organization. One of the usual starting points is to get together a group of interested managers, or in some instances managers and subordinates, to brainstorm various techniques for providing vertical loading. Participants in these sessions are asked for any ideas that might be applied to change the jobs, without any constraints or attempts to screen the practicality of the ideas. Anything at all goes. Typically, participants come up with a large number of ideas, which are listed in random order.

Following the idea-generation phase, the group is asked to screen the ideas. One approach is to first classify them into hygiene- (context-) related items as opposed to motivator (job content) factors. Then duplicate ideas and ideas that are completely unreasonable because of cost or other organizational considerations are eliminated. Finally, the ideas are evaluated in terms of ease of implementation and probable motivational impact, and a priority for implementing the changes is set up.

The next step should be assessment of the appropriateness of the ideas for the specific employees engaged in the jobs. A schedule for altering the jobs should be set up and concurrence with other people in the organization who will be affected needs to be achieved.

At this initial planning stage, it is important to set up the project evaluation strategy. Rather than trusting in some general belief that in fact something happens, it is important to be able to demonstrate just what happens, and this means an evaluation design. Usually similar measures before and after the job changes are used. A major aspect of adequate evaluation entails taking similar measures on a control group in which the nature of the job is not changed. Only by contrasting before and after measures in a group where changes are made with a similar group where changes are not made is it possible to say with assurance that changes in performance or attitudes really result from changes in job design.

It is also important that evaluations take into account the period of learning that almost without exception follows the implementation of job development concepts. Initially there probably will be some decline in performance as people learn the new task. Thus the test must be run long enough for the initial decrements to work themselves out.

The major purpose of a demonstration test is to provide a tangible example that can be used for "spreading the gospel." The results of the evaluation should be publicized and used to sell the concept. Reports on the project, presentations, and general discussions can be used to review the results of the test case and to suggest the extension of the concept to other areas of the business. Once an organization has gotten some key managers in the organization interested in and willing to support a job development test, has trained some key people, has successfully implemented a test program, and has actually placed some employees into enriched jobs, it is well on the way toward incorporating this important concept and methodology into its way of life. Such an organization now has a powerful tool for combating the winding down process.

References

1. F. L. W. Richardson, Jr. and C. R. Walker, *Human Relations in an Expanding Company* (New Haven: Yale University Press, 1948).
2. J. Gooding, "It Pays to Wake Up the Blue-Collar Worker," *Fortune*, September 1970, p. 158.
3. H. M. F. Rush, *Job Design for Motivation* (New York: National Industrial Conference Board, 1971).
4. R. N. Ford, *Motivation Through the Work Itself*, AMA, 1969, p. 180.
5. D. McGregor, *The Human Side of Enterprise* (New York: McGraw-Hill, 1960).
6. F. Herzberg, B. Mausner, and B. B. Snyderman, *The Motivation to Work* (New York: Wiley, 1959); F. Herzberg, *Work and the Nature of Man* (Cleveland: World Publishing Co., 1966).
7. R. N. Ford, op. cit.
8. ———— ,op. cit.
9. ———— , op. cit.

10. M. S. Myers, *Every Employee a Manager* (New York: McGraw-Hill, 1970).
11. E. D. Weed, Jr., "Job Enrichment 'Cleans Up' at Texas Instruments," Ch. 4 in J. R. Maher (ed.), *New Perspectives in Job Enrichment* (New York: Van Nostrand, 1971).
12. W. J. Paul Jr., K. B. Robertson, and F. Herzberg, "Job Enrichment Pays Off," *Harvard Business Review*, March–April, 1969.
13. IBM Corporation, "A Premise on Trial," *Think*, June 12, 1972.
14. "Management Itself Holds the Key," *Business Week*, September 9, 1972.
15. "Taking Boredom off the Assembly Line," *International Herald Tribune*, November 14, 1972.
16. H. M. F. Rush, op. cit.
17. "Management Itself Holds the Key," *Business Week*, September 9, 1972.
18. J. Gooding, op. cit.
19. F. D. Doyle, "Job Enrichment plus OD—A Two-Pronged Approach at Western Union," Ch. 10 in J. R. Maher (ed.), *New Perspectives in Job Enrichment* (New York: Van Nostrand, 1971).
20. W. N. Penzer, "Managing Motivated Employees," *Personnel Journal*, May 1971.
21. D. Sirota and A. D. Wolfson, "Job Enrichment: What Are the Obstacles?" *Personnel*, May–June 1972; "Job Enrichment: Surmounting the Obstacles," *Personnel*, July–August 1972.

10

ORGANIZATION DEVELOPMENT

IN THIS CHAPTER we shall focus on the third specific cluster of factors that determine the degree of an individual's commitment to his company and his job. These factors, which the employee encounters in his day-to-day working environment, affect his ability to get the job done. They are—

- Availability of information required to do the job, including the employee's knowledge of where to go to get information—and how.
- Clear perception of what is expected of him and what his job role is.
- Perceived limits to his authority.
- Bureaucratic constraints, such as inhibiting rules, regulations, procedures.
- Teamwork and the degree of cooperation from other organizational members in meeting shared objectives.

Here, the locus of the problem is outside the man himself. Organizational factors are different from the factors discussed in the previous chapters: (a) the individual's skills and abilities, opportunities for growth, and correct job placement, and (b) his actual assignment and the appropriateness of the demands and challenges the work presents. The factors associated with ability to get the job done are tied more to the system in which the individual operates. Thus a new element is introduced—the organization itself. To overcome the obstacles to job commitment caused by organizational factors, we must consider strategies and technologies for changing the basic operation of the organization.

As a distinct body of theory, method, and practice, organization development (OD) is relatively new. Its emergence as a profession with dedicated spokesmen and practitioners is also relatively new (it has evolved in the past 20 years, at most). Its most rapid development has been during the latter part of the 1960s. Clearly, however, the growth of organization development has been vigorous. Books and even series of books appear regularly, and an informal network of practitioners periodically exchange information and experiences.

As is true of any emerging field, it is not always clear where the boundaries of organization development lie. Much of this is deliberate. OD practitioners have tried to maintain an open approach. Their concern has been with making organizations more effective, both in achieving objectives and in being more satisfying, rewarding places in which to work. The practitioners have seen any point of leverage as fair game, have considered any approach or technique eligible for trial.

Most of what OD practitioners do is based on behavioral science knowledge and insights. But concepts from industrial engineering, economics, or information theory, for example, are used if they can be of help in achieving OD objectives. As with job enrichment, OD practitioners have wanted to keep the area open, recognizing quite correctly that different approaches may be most appropriate in different situations.

For example, Burke and Hornstein see organization development potentially concerned with such things as:

1. Team building, or working with existing organization units to build greater collaboration, cooperation, and mutual effort toward the attainment of shared objectives.
2. Intergroup problem solving through resolution of conflicts between various groups.
3. Techno-structural interventions, which are defined as changes in the technology or structure of organizations. These include the job enrichment efforts described previously, as well as concern over reward systems, reporting relationships, and personnel placement.
4. Data feedback as a means of providing information an organization needs to support its own self-correcting mechanisms.
5. Training, traditionally not thought of as part of organizational development, but willingly embraced by OD practitioners.
6. Any other techniques that can impact on the pro-

cesses by which organizations functions—for example, management by objectives or career development programs.[1]

Most organization development people have been primarily concerned with team building and intergroup problem solving. In addressing these issues, they have used data feedback and various training methods quite frequently. There has also been some very deliberate linkage of OD and job enrichment. For example, Western Union believes that either one by itself provides only a partial means to enhancing job commitment and that team building and job enrichment ideally complement each other.[2]

Such a broad-based approach probably will become commonplace, for it is increasingly obvious that organizational attributes are intimately interconnected and mutually supportive. Although in this book we speak of such separate components as personnel development or job development or organization development, they cannot operate in isolation. What is done in one area—for example, in job development—has an impact on other areas. As indicated previously, an employee who becomes accustomed to challenging, rewarding, and stimulating work will continue to demand it. He will not be content to put up with things that detract from his ability to do his job well—bureaucratic constraints, insensitive supervision, and poor teamwork. He will also begin to demand an opportunity to grow and to move ahead. Intervention in the design of jobs will spill over into other areas, which must also be attended to by any concerted program to enhance motivation.

The close interrelationship of organizational systems is particularly evident in the area of training, as was proved about 20 years ago by an evaluation of training in human relations.[3] Training in and of itself could be demonstrated to be effective, but the effects were negligible if not negative when the trainees went back to their jobs. The success of the training given the supervisors was critically dependent on the total organizational system in which they functioned. All indications are that concentration on training alone will have little effect on enhancing organizational effectiveness; the total system must be addressed.

The rest of this chapter discusses some of the reasons why organization development is important in a total program to enhance motivation and commitment in the current motivation crisis. We shall discuss where OD most profitably should focus its attention. In doing this, we shall draw on a recently developed comprehensive model of modern-day organizations. Then we shall describe some of the most widely used approaches and methods to organization development. Finally, we shall touch upon some strategies for carrying out organization development, including ways of implementing it and gaining acceptance of it.

WHERE DOES OD FIT?

Probably one of the most useful theoretical positions for describing organizations comes from a comprehensive, insightful series of research projects by Paul Lawrence and Jay Lorsch of Harvard University. Their research and theorizing provide a framework for understanding some of the essential attributes for successful organizations, how these may vary with the environment and objectives of the organization, and leverage points that can be used in the overall process of organization development.

Lawrence and Lorsch describe an organization as "the coordination of different activities of individual contributors to carry out planned transactions with the environment." [4] This definition contains the key components of their theoretical position: *planned transactions, differentiation of activities*, and *coordination to attain the organization's plans.*

The need for organization development comes about from the conflicts that arise in meeting the conflicting demands made on today's organizations.

First, organizations require what Lawrence and Lorsch term "differentiation." That is the extent to which subunits or groups in the organization have specialized goals, objectives, and methods of operation. The degree of necessary differentiation between groups depends on the environment in which the organization operates. The key factor of the environment is the degree of environmental certainty—the extent to which events in the environment are predictable, goals are clear-cut, effort is relatively short range in time, and the information required for group functioning is clear and certain. Where there is high environmental certainty, there is low necessity for differentiation.

In complex organizations characterized by change,

long time horizons, diffuse goals, and an unclear environment, there is an increasing need for differentiation, or specialization, among subgroups. The trend is obvious in large organizations today, with their distinct departments for research, development, marketing, manufacturing, and so on, each having highly different theories of expertise and orientation toward problems, goals, and objectives. Without differentiation, these functions could not be performed effectively.

On the other hand, in all organizations there is a need for integration, for all members to work together to enhance overall organizational goals. When individual efforts to carry out planned transactions of the total organization are not coordinated, the organization is not functioning effectively.

When there is low differentiation in an organization, integration is not a major problem. The formal structure and authority relationships of classic organizations can usually coordinate activities. But in highly differentiated organizations, something more is needed. There is a need for more shared information and more influence over events by all organization members. It is here that organizational development efforts are most applicable in attempts to increase the level of integration.

This model of highly differentiated organizations with a need for systematic attention to integration of its subparts fits many organizations today. Undoubtedly there is little coincidence that this growing number of highly differentiated organizations also parallels the growing motivation crisis. A direct attack on the problem of insuring integration must be made to combat the crisis. Organization development is the most promising new methodology available for the attack.

KEY INTERFACES

OD efforts may be appropriate at a number of interfaces, or points, at which transactions within and between organizations occur. There are the organization-to-environment interface, the group-to-group interface, and the individual-to-organization interface. Other interfaces can be identified, but these are the areas where OD efforts are usually concentrated.

One aspect of the organization-to-environment interface is concern with raw materials, markets, labor, capital, and the like. Organization development efforts tend not to emphasize those factors in themselves but focus more on the relationships of the organization and its ability to cope with change. Issues such as the sales department's relationship to markets, R&D's to technology, or administrative procedures and practices vis-à-vis changing values in society can be sources of conflict that call for OD attention. Usually problems at the organization-to-environment interface come about as a response to economic indicators. Perhaps R&D is not coming out with new products, competition is getting ahead, sales are falling off, or recruitment efforts are failing.

Problems at the group-to-group interface are often signaled by a general uneasiness about poor communications, lack of cooperation, or somebody's dropping the ball when a situation was assumed to be well in hand. The organization development effort is designed to focus on the integration efforts between groups to achieve collaboration, sharing of objectives, and open, fuller communication, and at the same time to maintain the necessary differentiation required for the task at hand.

Another area often addressed by OD is the individual-to-organization interface. Here the concern is to insure that processes and procedures maximally motivate the members of the organization. The issues involved in individual and job development operate at this interface. Some indications of problems in this area are high turnover, absenteeism, poor work quality, or declining morale. Here the objective of OD is to insure that jobs become more rewarding and satisfying to individuals by meeting their basic needs and personal goals.

The Focus of OD

One useful approach to understanding the focus of organization development is to compare it to the process of individual development. The process consists of all the factors that encourage and assist a person to sharpen his competence, to broaden his horizons, and to grow personally and advance in his career. Formal training is certainly a part of this, often a major part. Fully as important, however, are less tangible attributes such as on-the-job coaching, job rotation, specific task force assignments, special projects, and increasing responsibility. The actual development process is up to the individual, true development being self-development. The organization's responsibility is to provide the facilities, the opportunity, and the climate for personal growth. Within this framework, the growth process must be self-generated.

Similarly, the objectives of OD are to provide the climate, the information, and the methodology for a total organization to grow and mature. Formal training may be part of that methodology. Other formal techniques, such as organization design and job design, may also fit into the OD strategy. But the overall emphasis is on organizational self-development. The entire thrust of OD is to build a climate, to bring to bear tools and techniques, and to provide a catalyst for an organization to become aware of its own areas of effective and ineffective operations, as well as to counteract forces detracting from its effectiveness. OD is something that an organization should learn to do to itself, not something that is done to it.

Because organizations are aggregates of individuals, the primary area of emphasis in OD is to insure effective interaction between individuals or groups of individuals. The main OD objectives are to—

1. Provide a climate for genuine communication so that information flows openly and accurately and is available to all when needed. Openness and authenticity of communication are stressed. This implies the need for nonevaluative listening on the part of all concerned to achieve genuine understanding.
2. Build mutual trust throughout the organization. Openness of communication and nonevaluative listening can only be achieved in a climate where people trust one another.

3. Create an open, problem-solving climate throughout the organization so that all members are oriented toward overcoming the obstacles to effective functioning.

4. Increase in all employees their sense of "ownership" of the organization's objectives to enhance their motivation toward the attainment of those objectives.

5. Build a climate of mutual support among the members of the organization, including concern for the job welfare, growth, and personal success of one's peers.

6. Insure that responsibility for problem solving and decision making is delegated to the level of the organization where the optimal information and competencies are located.

7. Build authority based on knowledge and competence rather than purely on organizational role or status.

8. Increase self-control and self-direction rather than dependency for members of the organization.

9. Foster a climate of mutual respect for individual differences among organization members, one that stresses an adequate balance between group and individual approaches to problems.

10. Maximize collaborative efforts, at the same time recognizing the role of competition and shaping it to achieve the goals of the organization.

11. Accept the fact of conflict in organizations as normal, yet channeling it so that organizational effectiveness is not hampered.

12. Develop a reward system that recognizes the achievement of the organization's objectives as well as the development and growth of people.

13. Insure that the organization's management processes are based on relevant objectives rather than on tradition or parochial interest on the part of its officers.

OD Methodology

To achieve these rather broad objectives, the organization development movement has embraced a number of diverse methodologies. These go well beyond the traditional approaches of training or organizational design that formerly were the major tools employed in implementing changes. Although OD continues to use traditional methods, its broader approach to organizational change is the key to its effectiveness. One of the characteristics that distinguish OD from classic methods is its emphasis on employees' attitudes. The fact that negative feelings can detract from organizational effectiveness and positive feelings represent unused potential is implicit in most OD methodologies.

Another almost unique feature of OD is its heavy reliance on consultants or outside resources, at least in initial stages. The consultant's function is not necessarily to provide expert knowledge to the OD process, although this is sometimes the case. His main purpose is to provide objectivity and a broader frame of reference as organization members begin to examine the difficult areas of personal feelings and conflict. OD methodologies deal with conflict openly and constructively rather than suppress it. OD recognizes that interpersonal and intergroup conflict is inevitable in any organization but that the role of OD is to facilitate the management of conflict so that it contributes to organizational objectives. OD attempts to get around destructive competition, politics, parochialism, and so forth.

Through OD methodologies, responsibility for increasing organizational effectiveness is shared by all employees rather than entrusted solely to supervisors. There is a direct emphasis on building teamwork and coordinated commitment toward the attainment of organizational goals.

Another feature of OD is its use, to the extent possible, of internal resources in effecting change. Consultants are useful facilitators, but the long-range emphasis has to be on internal resources so that the change and development process becomes self-sustaining.

Finally, an orientation toward experimentation and a willingness to learn by failure as well as by success is part of the basic OD philosophy. The philosophy recognizes that there is no one fixed way to overcome barriers to organizational effectiveness and that by its very nature OD is a learning process. The methodologies stress the experimental aspect of organization development.

OD TECHNIQUES

Despite its relative newness, organization development has either adopted or developed a wide range of techniques to meet its objectives. Some of the more important techniques are discussed below.

Organization development usually is thought of as an

"intervention" into the normal functioning of an organizational system to unfreeze the existing sets of relationships, to provide skills, understanding, and commitment to adopt new sets of relationships, and to refreeze the organization into the newly developed system. While the ultimate objective is to provide the organization with the tools, climate, and insights to achieve this development on its own and maintain it as a continuing process, the initial approach is intervention on the part of an internal or external consultant who serves as a change agent. The evolution to a self-developing organization involves the gradual withdrawal of the change agent from the organizational system.

Typically, the intervention process is seen as going through several overlapping stages. Beer outlines the following.[5]

Diagnosis, which entails various techniques to determine which organizational problems need to be addressed and which practices and sets of relationships need to be modified to enhance organizational effectiveness.

Feedback to the organization members of the information obtained in the diagnosis is designed to achieve shared understanding of the problems and at the same time develop a feeling of "ownership" of the data and insights into the problems on the part of organization members. It is an active process to insure that organization members are committed to development and accept the diagnosis rather than view it as just something prepared by an outsider.

Action planning gets all the organization members involved in developing actions to overcome the problems uncovered in the diagnosis and communicated in the feedback stage. Action planning is also designed to obtain maximum commitment and ownership of action plans on the part of organization members.

Implementation is the carrying out of planned actions.

Evaluation is the diagnosis of the effectiveness of the action steps that were implemented, and perhaps leads back into another cycle of organization development to tune up those steps or to address additional problems.

The various techniques mentioned for carrying out these five stages of organization development may be cataloged under two basic orientations: diagnostic interventions and process interventions.

DIAGNOSTIC INTERVENTIONS

For a number of years social scientists and others have been using a variety of techniques to collect data about organizational functioning. These tools and techniques have been successfully used by OD specialists to diagnose problem areas. The diagnosis has then been fed into the organization as the basis for unfreezing and starting the change process. A diagnostic technique may consist of opinion and attitude questionnaires, interviews, evaluations of operating data from the organization (attrition, productivity, costs, and the like) and direct observations of organizational functioning. Often a number of these methods can be used in parallel. The data may be gathered by the outside consultant or by organization members.

In some instances particularly perceptive data about problems can be obtained through careful analysis of organizational problems by individuals who have just completed a T-group or sensitivity training experience. After a

T-group, organization members are usually very open and perceptive and have new information about blockages and supports to organizational effectiveness. If, as a group, they shift their frame of reference from the here and now of individual interpersonal effectiveness to the total organizational system, they frequently are able to generate considerable data about the problems an OD effort might profitably attack. A questionnaire or discussion may be used for collecting the data. This provides an excellent opportunity for bridging the gap from T-group participation to more effective interpersonal functioning in the organizational setting.

Data collection is an important but relatively easy aspect of the OD process. A somewhat more critical and difficult component is the feeding of data back into the management system in such a way that it is believable, timely, and relevant and is accepted and owned by the participants in the OD process. OD strategy contends that unless the participants really believe that the problems, and responsibility for solving them, are their own and within their capability to deal with, little change will take place. It is here where the outside consultant plays a critical role and where his skills, insights, and sensitivity are extremely important.

Data should be presented in group meetings so that the information is seen as pertinent to the group as a whole and becomes owned by the group in terms of responsibility for action. The group feedback of data and analysis of survey results also provide an opportunity for the group to understand the interactions taking place be-

tween individuals. The effectiveness of the group in decision making, collaboration, problem solving, and openness
can be assessed by the outside consultant and explained to
the group participants through a variety of techniques that
help them understand the key elements in group effectiveness. Feedback and discussion of interview results can
take place in a similar way.

A confrontation meeting is an effective technique for
handling the data-gathering and feedback phase. Here a
group of organizational members are given the responsibility for developing lists of key problems and for achieving very specific objectives. They then break into small
groups to discuss and clarify what they see as key problem
areas. These are presented to the larger group where the
inputs from each individual group are combined and categorized. Then new groups are formed to deal with problems in specific categories. They discuss the problems and
come up with action solutions and recommended timeta-
bles. Each group then feeds back its conclusions to the
larger group. A follow-up meeting to assess actions actually undertaken and their effectiveness is an important part
of the confrontation meeting. This procedure differs from
the data-gathering and feedback procedures outlined above
primarily in that group members themselves are involved
in both the identification of the problem and the development of action recommendations. Thus they gain a closer
understanding of the data and presumably have more commitment to act on it.

OD practitioners have used other techniques to
gather data and feed it back for subsequent use by organi-

zation members in initiating change. These include collecting data from key groups with which an organization unit has frequent contact (customers, suppliers, dependent departments), group problem solving by a "family group," or special channels to encourage upward communications, such as open door policies, executive interviews by key managers with individuals or groups of employees at the base of the organization, and formal question and answer sessions. Any technique that generates data and gets it to the level of the organization where it is relevant, believed, and accepted as a base for initiating change can be viewed as an appropriate OD diagnostic intervention tool. Frequently, as we have said, more than one technique will be used at a particular time.

Implicit in all data gathering and feedback is the follow-on stage of action planning and goal setting to initiate change. Unless there is commitment to do something, the diagnostic intervention is a pointless exercise. In fact, without the action follow-through, such interventions typically do more harm than good by frustrating expectations for positive change, raising questions about the credibility of management commitment to change, and sensitizing people to problems without providing relief. The action-planning, goal-setting, and follow-through stage is vital. In OD it is the direct reflection of the prior commitment of the organization, and most specifically of top management, to complete the full cycle of the OD process. There must be a commitment to change before embarking on the diagnostic and feedback phase. When this is so, the action-planning, goal-setting, implementation, and evaluation stages will flow naturally.

PROCESS INTERVENTIONS

These techniques, which get at the basic functioning of the organization, are designed to evaluate the ongoing work environment, provide awareness of problems, and generate action planning and implementation of change. They build naturally on the diagnosis and feedback techniques.

When one thinks about techniques designed to examine interpersonal relations, which is a primary objective of process interventions, the first technique that comes to mind is the T-group, or sensitivity training. Over the past 20 years T-groups have become so well known and have been applied in such a variety of settings that they often are thought of as synonymous with process intervention in organizations.

That is a gross overextension of the role and potential of T-groups in organization development. Not that the T-group is ineffective for OD purposes. But it has only limited uses. In OD, process interventions are more concerned with assessing the effectiveness of ongoing relationships in an organization and trying to improve them to enhance the attainment of organizational goals. T-groups, on the other hand, are designed to provide individuals with awareness, understanding, and sensitivity. The goal is to help individuals to function more effectively in interpersonal settings. True, this may have implications for organizational processes, but the actual objectives of the T-group itself are more limited. In fact, research on T-groups suggests that the same problems inherent in training in general plague the transfer of learning from a T-group back to an organizational setting. Quite often, the individual gains new awareness and sensitivity, but when he tries to operate back in his home company in the mode he has learned in the T-group, it is an alien world. He very quickly realizes that behaviors appropriate in a T-group are often inappropriate in the typical unfrozen organization.

Precisely because of these problems the concept of organization development has evolved. The focus is on extending the concern with process within a T-group to a concern with process within a total system. Presumably, if awareness of the implications of interpersonal functioning for the attainment of organizational objectives can be built up in an ongoing system, there would be more receptivity to transfer the insights from T-groups back to the organization.

A T-group can be an important part of organization development, usually as a preliminary step to process interventions in the total organization. It can be a technique for providing individual organization members with an orientation toward sensitivity and an awareness of some of the concepts and processes of group dynamics. Awareness at the individual level may be a useful base for transferring awareness to the total organizational level. So T-groups definitely are used in organization development. But it should be recognized that they are artificial and temporary situations with relatively limited potential for maintaining the norms of the T-group in the organization without further process intervention. This is the important added dimension that OD specialists have brought to the entire sensitivity training movement, which recently has gained so much attention in industry and other settings.

One very common method for process intervention is the use of an outside consultant to process meetings. This means that the consultant sits in on ongoing staff meetings to observe the participants' interactions and how they contribute to or inhibit the effective functioning of the meeting. He provides feedback to participants, either during the meeting or at its conclusion, and on a group or individual basis. Tape recordings and videotapes of the meetings can be a powerful tool in providing feedback. The procedure depends heavily on the willingness of the individuals to accept the consultant's observations and on his skill and experience in observation, analysis, and communication. But the analysis during ongoing meetings probably is the most direct and most practiced form of process intervention in organization development.

An extension of the technique of processing meetings is the concept of team development. Here a consultant works with a primary work group that has a common mission to attain. Team development consists of, first, gathering data about group process and the problems associated with the specific team. The data can be obtained through questionnaires or interviews or by any method that seems appropriate. Information may be sought about any aspect of interpersonal functioning, such as communications, trust, leadership, rules, and decision making. When the data are available, the total team meets, usually off site so that they are away from day-to-day problems. The data about process within the team are then worked through with the consultant, and problems are categorized, discussed, and given priority. Throughout this process, the objective is to make the group "process-aware" so that in future interactions the problems can be identified and dealt with more openly rather than smoothed over and suppressed.

Four basic types of team development interventions can be identified:[6]

The goal-setting model. The objectives are for the team to identify their common goals and to develop commitment toward their attainment, integrating individual goals into group goals.

The interpersonal model. The primary objective is to develop effective interpersonal relations within the total team.

The role model. Different roles in which individuals operate are explored, and conflicts associated with the interactions of individual roles in the team are evaluated and dealt with.

The Managerial Grid® model. Based on Managerial Grid® theory, it uses various instruments and data-gathering techniques to assess individuals' views about the degree of cooperation from each member of a group and how it enhances or detracts from group effectiveness. Then the Grid® framework is used in overcoming the barriers to group effectiveness and building team cohesion.

Team development generally uses a combination of techniques and methods. Certainly in trying to clarify individual goals and integrate them into group goals and objectives, one has to explore roles and one also becomes concerned with interpersonal functioning. The Managerial

Grid® model also includes components of other models. Thus team development should be viewed as a broad-based effort to facilitate the functioning of ongoing teams by working at the individual, the interpersonal, and the total group level. Like the technique of processing meetings, team development depends to a considerable extent on the skills, insights, and experiences of the consultant who serves as the catalyst.

Another type of process intervention is the resolution of intergroup conflicts. This entails providing integration to an organization where there is necessary differentiation of functions, as our discussion of the organizational model early in this chapter showed. Intergroup intervention is designed to help groups deal with conflict productively, not necessarily to prevent it. The process is based on the assumption that within differentiated organizations, individual groups have individual missions, objectives, modes of operation, and needs. When one group has contact with another group with different patterns of needs and objectives and when their rewards or operations are to some extent interdependent, a certain amount of conflict is inevitable.

The most typical form of intergroup conflict in most organizations is win–lose conflict. Here the focus of intergroup relations is on trying to beat out the other group, to get ahead of it, to put it down. The framework is "us versus them." The problem with win–lose conflict is that, if unchecked, it becomes self-perpetuating and self-fulfilling. Individuals in the other group are seen as the cause of the conflict and as somehow malicious. The process tends to reinforce itself so that only the good parts of "our group" and the worst parts of the "other group" are perceived. Then the relations between the groups deteriorate into a conflict situation.

Intergroup process intervention is designed to identify this tendency, give each group feedback about how the other group perceives it, provide an understanding of the objectives and roles of the other group, diagnose problems in the interaction of the two groups, and develop action plans for improving relations to the extent possible. Most frequently, a laboratory format has been used, with the actual groups working together at an off-site location. Intergroup laboratories are particularly useful and have been tried in areas such as relations between different functional groups in industry, between labor and management representatives, between participants in a new acquisition or merger, and between contractors and subcontractors.

A variety of other techniques used by organization development specialists can be thought of as process interventions. They include such things as interpersonal peacemaking in which the consultant, either on a one-to-one or a group basis, tries to resolve conflicts between individuals. Counseling or individual guidance may be used to help individuals deal with problems that seem to be blocking group effectiveness. Sometimes temporary task forces can be useful in developing a new approach for dealing with specific problems and in trying to overcome barriers to organizational effectiveness. Temporary task forces in general are not too powerful, however; because they are not permanent, their influence on an ongoing process may be transitory.

In addition to diagnostic or process interventions OD specialists include a number of other techniques within their area of concern. They feel perfectly free to use things like job design or job enrichment if they will contribute to total organizational effectiveness. Also, direct concern for the total organization per se is seen as within their scope—including overall personnel systems, pay systems, staffing systems, organization structure and roles, and financial and budgeting control systems. This broad base is in keeping with OD orientation, which is very open, eclectic, and flexible. OD practitioners see their charter as being able to employ a wide range of methodologies and techniques, with points of entry anywhere in an organization, to help improve the effectiveness of the total system in achieving its objectives. Most typically, practitioners employ several techniques rather than take a single approach to the organization development process.

IMPLEMENTING OD INTERVENTIONS

One of the more important attributes of OD is its recognition that there is no single, optimal approach to achieving its objectives. But, with ten or more years of experience behind them, practitioners have developed some strategies or general orientations that form a framework for effective implementation of OD techniques. A "how to do it" discussion is beyond the scope of this book, but an overview of these strategies is useful for further understanding the process. The following list includes some of the main points useful to follow in implementing OD.*

- OD is not a packaged program; it is flexible in style and should be tailored to fit the problem, the people in the organization, and the consultant.
- The data are owned by the members of the organization. They are the primary agents in collecting, diagnosing, interpreting, and acting on their problems.
- The total team is involved in the process (to insure organizational relevancy and ownership of data).
- A consultant or consultants facilitate the process by representing a model of behavior, by feeding back to the group how they are interacting, and by offering specific techniques to suggest new forms of behavior. The consultant is not a problem solver; his function is to help the group deal with as much data as they are ready to receive.
- Participants are encouraged to examine and comment on group process.
- The processes initiated by OD techniques have no end. No organization can be "through with it once and for all."
- Results can be expected only after what may seem a long period of time. The length of time depends on the problem, the group's level of development, and external factors.
- The level of discourse is primarily practical rather than theoretical.

* *This list was compiled by Dr. L. A. Mischkind, Personnel Research Department, IBM, San Jose, Calif.*

- The effort eventually involves managers, non-managers, and individual employees.
- OD efforts require the continuous involvement and interest of the top man or men in a given subunit.

Recently several of the most seasoned OD consultants recorded their experiences and techniques.[7] That discussion of the dynamics of OD, various strategies and models, process consultation, role of the consultant, and attributes of an effective OD specialist provides important background material.

As valuable as that background information may be, however, the only truly effective way of learning how to do it is by actually getting involved. The potentials for OD are enormous. The need for it is large. As organizations become more and more complex and as the problems detracting from motivation and contributing to the winding down process become more pervasive, we will need more and more people skilled in the methodologies and techniques of organization development. And we can expect new methodologies to be developed to supplement the already powerful set of techniques available in this important area.

REFERENCES

1. W. W. Burke and H. A. Hornstein, *Introduction to the Social Technology of Organization Development* (not yet published).
2. F. P. Doyle, "Job Enrichment plus OD-A Two-Pronged Approach at Western Union," Ch. 10 in J. R. Maher (ed.), *New Perspectives in Job Enrichment* (New York: Van Nostrand, 1971).
3. E. A. Fleischman, E. H. Harris, and H. E. Burtt, "Leadership and Super-

vision in Industry," Ohio State Business Education Monograph, No. 3, 1955.

4. P. R. Lawrence and J. W. Lorsch, *Developing Organizations: Diagnosis and Action* (Reading, Mass.: Addison-Wesley Publishing Co., 1969), p. 3.

5. M. Beer, "The Technology of Organization Development," in M. Dunnette (ed.), *Handbook of Industrial and Organizational Psychology* (New York: Rand McNally), in press.

6. Ibid.

7. Addison-Wesley series on organization development (Reading, Mass.: Addison-Wesley, 1969).

ORGANIZING FOR THE FUTURE

INTRODUCTION

WE CITED some rather compelling evidence that there is in fact a motivation crisis in American industry. The existence of the crisis has been well documented. It pervades all areas of business and industry. It is serious. And when other clear trends in the economy and in the society at large are considered, there is little reason to expect the crisis to evaporate on its own. It is a problem that demands action.

The potential implications of the problem, unless corrected, are relatively clear. At the level of the individual organization or company, a motivation crisis of the scope we have discussed points clearly to declining efficiency of operation, increased costs, lower productivity, inability to compete in open markets, inflexibility, and unadaptability to change—in net, a stagnant organization. At the level of the individual employee, the crisis suggests wasted human potential, dissatisfaction, unfulfillment of personal goals and objectives, alienation, lack of purpose, and declining self-esteem—a significant impact on individuals with clear implications for the mental health, happiness, and well-being of the society at large. At the level of the total society, a motivation crisis of the magnitude that seems to exist suggests declining growth, loss of technological edge for the national economy, increasing difficulty in competing in world markets, with all its implications for balance of payment, national prestige, and so on. If allowed to continue, the motivational malaise will have far-reaching effects on our total society and way of life.

We have also pointed to three major directions an organization must consider if it wishes to attack the motivation crisis. They focus on three levels:

1. Efforts to enhance the development of individual employees.
2. Efforts to enhance the development of their jobs, and
3. Methodologies and techniques to enhance ongoing relations between people and groups in organizations.

Each area of activity is extremely important in combating the motivation crisis; all three will have to be used in a coordinated program.

But by themselves these three lines of effort still will not turn the situation around. Something more is needed. This something more is a rather drastic overhaul of the fundamental structure of most organizations. There are pervasive indications that many of the components of organization systems today will be inadequate for providing motivation tomorrow. It is extremely questionable that any program of individual, job, or organization development can correct motivation problems if the programs are expected to operate in an outdated organizational framework.

This section will outline some general directions of changes in traditional organizational forms that appear to be called for. Then we shall consider specific recommendations for new organizational relationships that should tie in more closely with the motivational needs of today's employees and suggest a framework for maintaining the vitality of tomorrow's organizations.

11

NEW ORGANIZATION FORMS FOR TOMORROW'S NEEDS

THE FORMS characteristic of most industrial and business organizations today evolved relatively recently. It was only with the advent of the industrial revolution during the eighteenth and nineteenth centuries that a need for formal industrial organizations arose. In the previous years of cottage industries and craftsmen, organization was clearly not a problem. But when groups of people were brought together into commercial enterprises, some way had to be found to coordinate their activities, to achieve organizational effectiveness, and to insure continuation of the enterprise.

As these organizations were being designed, it was only natural to borrow organizational concepts from the two major organizations then in existence—the Roman Catholic Church and the military. Because both the Church and the military organizations had been around for centuries and had prospered, evolving industrial organizations very deliberately patterned themselves after these two institutions.

The terms and concepts still used to describe current-day organizations reflect this origin. We continue to talk about line versus staff, span of control, chain of command, hierarchy, rewards and punishments as incentives, unity of command, subordinates reporting to superiors, loyalty, authority, dedication, and so forth. Such concepts clearly might have been appropriate in newly formed organizations at the beginning of the industrial revolution. It is not at all clear, however, that they continue to be useful. But they have become so thoroughly entrenched in the framework of modern management theory and practice that they are taken as almost universal principles of organization. As such, only rarely have they been questioned. It is only quite recently that a few authors and theorists have begun to present alternate possibilities for organizing industrial enterprises. But it is even less frequent that any of these alternate forms are actually tried in ongoing organizations.

In the face of the current motivation crisis, we desperately need a whole range of creative new approaches to organizing a productive enterprise. We need the willingness to experiment with these new approaches. We need a systematic evaluation of those experiments so that we may build a body of knowledge for improving the design of organizations. If we do not make significant advances the crisis will get out of hand.

Again, this is not to say there has not been some amount of new organization theory and technique, experimentation, and testing throughout the relatively short history of industrial organizations. The organization of today differs in some significant aspects from the organization of

200 years ago. But the development of organization theory and principles and techniques is still built on the original foundation borrowed from the Catholic Church and the military. Because these worked well, "innovation" has consisted of refining the system. Very specifically the "classic" organization theorists such as Urwick or Fayol drew on such military-based concepts as line versus staff functions in developing the theories of management that have held sway for the past 50 years.

BUREAUCRACY AND SCIENTIFIC MANAGEMENT

Two other schools of thought have played an extremely important role in determining the shape of present-day management and organization theory—bureaucracy and scientific management.

The concept of bureaucracy originated with the German sociologist Max Weber. His contribution was to define an ideal organization as one that would overcome all the prevalent problems of favoritism, nepotism, and discrimination characteristic of many organizations in the late nineteenth century. To do this, he set down some clear principles of organizaton that have had a profound impact on current organization structures. Basically what Weber said was that there should be clear rules of organization to determine how incumbents in the middle management positions of large organizations behaved. These bureaucrats were seen as the individuals between the top leadership of an organization and the rank-and-file employees. It was their function to carry out the directions of the leadership and to control the activities of the rank and file. In doing this, Weber believed, they should follow a number of principles designed to maximize the efficiency of the organization's functioning and to insure against the old practices of favoritism, personal prejudice, and irrationality in earlier organizational forms.

Weber's standards for effective bureaucratic behavior maintained that—

- There should be a clear division of responsibility among the different offices of the organization. This would be accomplished by position descriptions and formal charts of organization to clarify who is responsible for what.
- The structure of the organization should be hierarchical, with each member of the organization responsible to one superior. The individual would be responsible to his superior for his own actions, as well as for those of his subordinates.
- A clear system of rules should be set down to insure uniformity and coordination in the execution of tasks. This means there would be a clearly delineated, correct way for each task to be performed. Individuals would be appointed to offices on the basis of technical competence, determined to the extent possible by means of objective criteria such as examinations and seniority.
- There should be emphasis on security, with lifetime tenure and pension rights guaranteed, fixed incremental salaries, and formal promotion procedures.
- There should be a "social distance" between the

manager and his subordinates, and the employee's personal life should not be subject to organizational sanctions. Clear controls and sanctions would, however, be exercised in the work environment.

In many circles the term "bureaucracy" is a bad word; somehow it has become associated with great inefficiency, often in government offices. But in fact, as originally conceived by Weber, bureaucracy was the height of efficiency and was designed very deliberately to make organizations rational, to protect employees from unreasonable or capricious actions, and to provide security. The bureaucratic model has been relatively successful in achieving those objectives, and the main aspects of bureaucracy are still found in almost all organizations today: division of labor, hierarchical structure, clarity of rules, objective impersonalism, orientation to rules, and concern with security. Certainly not all these per se are bad or inefficient. But in excess, and in the wrong setting, they may be.

The second refinement to early organizational systems was accomplished through the scientific management school. Here, largely on the basis of the work of Frederick Taylor and his associates early in the twentieth century, several basic principles for designing the most efficient organization were developed. These include—

1. Breaking a job down into its smallest component set of tasks.
2. Studying each task to determine what is the one best way to perform it.
3. Placing people in the jobs for which they have the

correct attributes and aptitudes and training them how to do it in the one best way.

4. Controlling the way in which the job is done, placing time limits on it, compensating on the basis of output through some piece rate system, and supervising performance closely.

The main thrust of the scientific management approach, like that of bureaucracy, is still found in most organizations today.

PROBLEM AREAS

It is only within the past few years that we have begun to question the traditional structure of organization. There are several reasons for our questions. First, managers are beginning to take seriously some of the research findings and theory evolving from the behavioral sciences. Particularly over the past 20 years a tremendous amount of research knowledge has been generated about such important organizational areas as motivation, communication, leadership, job satisfaction, incentive, and personal development. Much of the research has highlighted the constraining aspects of many traditional assumptions about people and organizations.

At the same time, practical people have found that the traditional system is working less effectively. This awareness has become almost universal in the face of the motivation crisis as we have defined it in this book.

As a result of this research and insight, we can now point to a number of specific problem areas.

Traditional sources of authority no longer function as they used to. Formal power was the mechanism used to control employees. It was legitimate and accepted. Power was viewed as the innate right of the organization to determine conditions of work, to direct, to reward, to punish. Employees were controlled through the exercise of power—hired, fired, assigned, promoted, paid, and so forth. This concept of power inevitably built conflict into the relation between employees and the organization. The organization functioned to enhance the owners' objectives, which did not necessarily agree with those of the employees.

Now, however, no organization has a free hand in exercising economic power over its employees. Hiring, firing, and compensating have been more and more limited by the role of organized labor, government regulations, legislation, and the norms of enlightened organizational operations.

The other traditional source of power derived from the work ethic. Employees accepted the right of organizations to control operations, to determine the conditions of work, to insist on a full day's work for a full day's pay. This source of power has been extremely strong throughout the history of industrial organizations. In the recent past, it probably has been the major source of power for organizations to rely on in the virtual absence of economic power.

The work ethic is now being strongly challenged. As work values are changing and as the legitimacy of organizations and authority are being questioned, this last source of power to control employees is eroding.

One of the biggest needs in today's organizations is

for a new definition of power relationships—new forms and procedures of organization designed to equalize power and to help power to be perceived as legitimate.

The hierarchical system tends to build conformity into an organization. It makes the subordinate depend on the superior for approval, direction, and information. Such dependency relationships have been found to inhibit creative expression. Employees learn not to take risks and not to make suggestions that may in any way be viewed by superiors as a criticism of the status quo. Relationships become rigid, growth is inhibited, employees become passive. Formal hierarchical relationships are not associated with a dynamic, adaptive, creative organization.

Hierarchical relationships tend to undermine employees' self-esteem. Research study after research study has shown that one of the most important correlates of motivated, productive, creative performance is a strong sense of self-esteem. The dependency relationships that evolve from traditional authority structures usually are demeaning to the self-image of subordinates.

Traditional authority structures tend to be inflexible. The myriad rules, red tape, levels of review and approval, and the like result in hardening of the organizational arteries. The inflexibility of traditional structures is reflected in all the jokes and stereotypes about large, bureaucratic organizations (often government bodies). In today's rapidly changing environment hardening of the arteries certainly will cripple, if not destroy, an organization's ability to function.

The functional division of labor, if carried to the extreme, tends to inhibit creativity. When people are divided into overly homogeneous groups to perform clearly defined, narrow functions, procedures become standardized and everyone starts to think alike. A necessary condition for change, adaptability, and creativity is a diversity of viewpoints from people with different backgrounds and orientations.

Traditionally, organizations have assigned people to jobs on an open-ended, permanent basis. The practice has been, following on concepts developed from classic bureaucratic theory, to define a specific task to be done and then to assign an individual to do it. He remains in that position for an indefinite period, perhaps for his total career. The only way he will move is if the organization finds another position for which it feels he has the appropriate qualifications. (Very rarely does an organization try to find or tailor a job to qualify for an individual's needs.) Our discussion of winding down and job decay indicated how dangerous this practice can be. There is natural job decay, which practically guarantees that in time an individual in a permanent assignment will become increasingly dissatisfied and lose his motivation. It is also becoming more and more evident that people are demanding more personal control over their assignments. Jobs need to be shaped to people rather than people to jobs. Jobs need to be thought of as not permanent but as temporary and variable. Some new forms to achieve those objectives need to be designed.

Narrow specialization is just plain inefficient. With more and more highly qualified, trained people entering the workforce, traditional job design just does not use the full skills and abilities people bring to work. The problem is getting worse. More flexibility in jobs and assignments needs to be built systematically into organizational systems to insure that people are able to fully use their skills.

These are just some of the problem areas that are very evident in traditional organizations. There is clearly a need for change. No doubt some of these changes will evolve naturally. There already has been some change in many organizations, or at least there has been a growing awareness of the need for change and of the problems in the current system.

Stronger effort is required, however, to respond adequately to the motivation crisis. A quote from *Business Week* sums it up nicely:

> Organization structures are creaking under today's pressures. Something is out of synchronization. Patterned after the way a Prussian General ran his army in the 1850's, the organization charts more and more reveal shortcomings. The rigid organization lines and authoritarian style of that era seem increasingly out of touch with reality.[1]

Approaches to Changing Organization Forms

As the problem has become more widely recognized, specific recommendations for change have come from a number of quarters. Some of these are from men of ideas—people interested in the theory of organizations—psychologists, sociologists, and the like. Some are from men of action—businessmen, applied social scientists attempting to change organizations, and so forth. Some are merely statements of desired directions for change, sometimes sounding more like wishful thinking than concrete actions that an ongoing organization can implement readily. Some represent actual, tremendously successful implementations of new organization systems. A sample of these suggestions may provide a flavor of the changes currently being considered.

For example, Abraham Korman, an industrial psychologist, devoted a chapter of his book to the problems inherent in traditional forms of organization.[2] He outlined the factors that should be considered in restructuring an organization. His approach does not advocate complete overhaul; Korman recognizes some of the real benefits existing in the traditional model: need for rationality when decisions must be made quickly, desirable orderliness and predictability of the traditional system, efficiency when production is not under the control of the individual, clarity of the rules of behavior. But, Korman argued, the constraints to productivity and creativity from the dependency relationships and inflexibility of traditional systems suggest the following revisions.

1. To overcome the effects of dependency and to promote creativity in the organization, idea men should be hired with the sole responsibility of providing innovative ways of approaching and developing answers to problems.

2. Individuals who are explicitly "different" from those traditionally hired should also be employed, to insure that new ideas are brought into the organization.

3. Management control should be focused on monitoring the final outcomes of work rather than the way in which the work is done, in order to increase the self-esteem of the employee and his sense of competence.

4. There should be increased rotation among jobs, and an expectation that people will develop and grow into

new jobs. This should help enhance their own self-confidence, sense of growth, and provide more heterogeneity within work groups, which should enhance creativity. The objective is to build a more fluid organization.

5. More participation by employees in decision making should be encouraged, through formal plans such as the Scanlon plan and multiple management. Employees should be involved more in the planning of work and decisions about how it will be carried out, with rewards (bonuses and profit sharing, for example) associated with effective performance.

6. Systems to encourage the input of new ideas to management and upward communications should be put into effect. Any kind of program that will encourage innovation from the bottom of the organization and overcome dependency relationships should be employed.

7. Professionalism should be encouraged so that people identify with a group outside the specific organization, to avoid using the organization's norms as the sole criteria in self-evaluation.

8. The formal control and evaluation inherent in most organizations today should be reduced to the extent possible. This again is designed to overcome dependency relationships in hierarchical organizations.

9. New ideas should be evaluated to the extent possible on the merits of their content rather than on "who" suggested them.

10. Project teams should be used where feasible. There are two aspects to this suggestion. First, temporary teams should be set up where desirable to deal with specific projects or problems. This is the task force approach.

The task force may continue with the project only to some specified point of completion, or it may be a continuing committee with rather long-range responsibilities. The second aspect of project teams is what has become known as the matrix form of organization. Here, representatives of different functions affected by a problem are assigned to the team and given equal responsibility and authority. Thus the traditional hierarchical system is replaced by a more fluid, dynamic, ad hoc unit with multiple interfaces and relationships. One advantage of a matrix organization is the heterogeneity in composition of the project teams, which tends to enhance creativity and learning.

11. A formal system of "consumer representation" should be built into the structure. This means that people who are serviced by the organization, whether within the organization or outside, should have some voice in planning what the organization does. There should be a systematic mechanism to provide feedback from consumers on "customer satisfaction" so that the organizational unit may correct problems as they occur.

12. The performance appraisal process should not include only the traditional superior–subordinate discussion. It should also contain self-appraisal and appraisals by peers. This method will provide a more complete evaluation and a broader perspective.

13. There should be an effort to decrease the number of supervisory levels in the hierarchy to encourage independence and self-control and to remove some of the bureaucratic constraints to organizational effectiveness. This means very specifically trying to "flatten" the organization's structure.

Most of these suggestions by Korman are not particularly radical. They tend to focus on the individual–organizational relationship. As a group, however, the suggestions could go a long way toward overcoming many of the negative effects of the traditional organization system.

More radical suggestions for change have been made by J. W. Forrester, a professor at M.I.T.[3] Forrester's background is in the physical sciences, but he has become increasingly interested in and recognized as an authority in administration. Among Forrester's proposals for a new corporate design are the following.

1. *Elimination of the superior–subordinate relationship.* Here Forrester envisions substituting self-control and self-discipline for the traditional superior–subordinate hierarchy system. He would do this by setting up a system in which each individual is essentially an entrepreneur. He must sell his services in competition with other organization members and other services available from outside the organization. His rewards should be based on the extent to which he is able to sell his services; in effect he becomes his own manager.

2. *Installation of individual profit centers.* The budget system is the traditional approach to financial control in an organization. Budgetary financial control almost inevitably leads to inflated budgets, hoarding of resources and manpower, a concerted effort to spend all of this year's budget because next year's budget is based on expenditures, and continuing conflict between the person who monitors the budget (the controller) and individual managers. The profit center approach puts the incentive on efficiency. Ac-

tivities and resources become valued in terms of profit—the difference between the input costs and a sale price that will be accepted in a competitive market. Future organization systems should enhance the profit center concept throughout an organization by basing both financial and psychological rewards on profits rather than control of expenditures. The profit center concept has to apply to small enough units so that it applies to individual managers; in most organizations profit centers tend to exist only in large units, and the impact on the behavior of individuals is limited.

3. *Objective determination of compensation.* Under a profit center system in which individuals are expected to sell their services in the organization, compensation can be based on results achieved (profits attained). Such an objective system should help remove the dependency relationship and negative implications for self-esteem from traditional hierarchical systems.

4. *Separation of policy making and decision making.* Forrester feels that in many organizations policy development and decision making are too closely intertwined. The role of policy is to provide a framework in which decisions can be made. Policy should be as unambiguous and unrestrictive as possible.

5. *Freedom of access to information.* Forrester suggests that all information be available very broadly throughout the organization rather than be restricted to specific individuals. This would be done partly through restructuring of electronic data processing systems and comprehensive evaluation of the information networks and needs of the organization. With more openness of information, depen-

dency relationships will be reduced, less effort will be lost with people trying to get information that is deliberately withheld from them, the irrationality and inequities associated with many practices currently cloaked in secrecy (for example, salary administration) will be evident and subject to correction.

6. *Elimination of internal monopolies.* It should be possible to buy services of all kinds from multiple sources, either within the organization or outside. The rationale behind this is the same as that of limiting monopoly in the national society—to insure maximum efficiency of the competitive system.

7. *Encouragement of mobility.* Systems should be set up to encourage mobility, at least mobility out of the organization. The retaining effects of pension funds and stock options tend to discourage people from leaving; they hold people for the wrong reasons. Maintenance of employment should be voluntary rather than result from financial coercion.

8. *Enhancement of individuals' rights.* Formal systems and an organizational "constitution" should be set up to protect the rights of individuals. This is particularly pertinent in technical and managerial ranks; production workers have already obtained some degree of protection through the trade union movement.

9. *Support of continued education.* Continued education could be looked on as an integral part of corporate life, systematically built into the system.

Forrester's list of suggested new organization forms contains some interesting potential innovations that possibly can have a major effect on reducing the negative aspects of traditional forms. So far, very few of his suggestions have been subjected to test. They warrant experimentation.

CASE STUDY

Before opening a new pet food processing plant, a large manufacturer spent considerable time developing a design to overcome worker alienation, dissatisfaction, and low productivity.[4] The key features of the design were:

1. Autonomous work groups were established. The workforce was organized into separate teams of 7 to 14 operators, with a team leader for each group. The team's responsibilities included a series of interdependent tasks that had to be tied together into the major component of the plant's operations. Team consensus determined the assignments of specific tasks to team members; movement between tasks was encouraged and depended only on the consensus of team members.

2. Support functions not ordinarily thought of as directly part of the manufacturing process were also performed by the team. These functions included such activities as screening employment applicants, housekeeping, work planning, and quality control.

3. The tasks assigned to individuals were designed to be as challenging as possible. As much of the dull, routine work as possible was automated, and responsibilities for planning, diagnosing mechanical or process problems, and liaison work were assigned to the operators. They did assume responsibility for some menial work, such as house-

keeping, to avoid having "second-class citizens" within the plant assigned exclusively to such nonchallenging work. The emphasis was very deliberately on insuring that all jobs demanded a certain amount of brainpower and presented challenge.

4. Job mobility and rewards for learning were encouraged. Pay raises were based on increasing acquisition of competence rather than movement up the heirarchy. Basic job levels and pay rates revolved around mastering an individual task, then mastering all tasks assigned to the team, and then mastering all tasks in the total plant. The reward system encouraged broadening one's skills, gaining an understanding of the total manufacturing process, and developing the ability to perform different tasks.

5. The team leader's role was to insure team development and to act as moderator in group decision making, rather than to directly plan and control activities. The expectation was that eventually the teams might become self-governing and the formal team leader position might not be required.

6. The operators were given financial and performance data ordinarily available only to management, as well as managerial decision rules, so that they themselves could make the necessary production decisions.

7. No formal rules of operation were set down when the plant was established. Management decided that the plant community should be self-governing and that such rules should evolve on the basis of experience.

8. Status symbols and differential treatment of workers were eliminated. Such things as preferential parking

facilities, separation of office from plant facilities, different cafeteria facilities, and other status symbols were avoided.

9. There was management commitment to learn from the system, to experiment, and to evolve new systems as the need arose.

The experience of this particular plant is especially important because the experience was real, something actually was done. The innovations were all in the direction of providing more autonomy for individual workers, more job challenge, more mobility, and more responsibility. The steps taken went a long way toward overcoming many of the negative effects of traditional organization forms. Most important, the innovations apparently have been extremely effective. The commitment and dedication of workers in the plant are high. Problems of alienation found in other manufacturing environments are nowhere nearly as prevalent. The plant was able to open with significantly fewer employees than had been forecast by engineering studies. Productivity and quality have been high. As a result of these very dramatic positive effects, the parent organization is expanding these concepts to many of its other manufacturing areas. It is a safe bet that this organization's competitors will have to start thinking along similar lines if they want to remain competitive over the years to come.

A Prototype Organization Form

Where do these various suggestions leave us? What is the mechanism by which they can be translated into tangible changes in the typical industrial organization we know today? What will a prototype organization system for the future look like? We shall attempt to outline one such prototype in an effort to pull together into a concrete framework these various suggestions. We shall also try to build into this new framework structures and directions that will enhance efforts to overcome the motivation crisis. It is a relatively radical proposal and perhaps it won't work. But it is a proposal that deserves serious study, elaboration, and testing. The need is too great and the crisis too important not to think and act in broad new directions; hopefully this model will stimulate additional thought and action in devising new organization forms.

The most logical point for implementing the type of system we shall outline is at the middle levels of medium to large organizations. These are the levels where bureaucracy presides. It is the point where most of the hardening of the arteries in today's organizations is taking place. Therefore, probably the most fruitful point of entry would be in a large headquarters organization. But similar concepts can be extended to other areas such as research, development, manufacturing, even marketing.

In contrast to bureaucracy, we call this concept *adhocracy.** There are four main thrusts to adhocracy:

1. The hierarchical, bureaucratic structure should be reduced to an absolute minimum (but not eliminated).

* *The contributions of a number of colleagues at IBM in developing this concept is acknowledged, specifically those of William Alper, Richard Dunnington, William Penzer, David Sirota, and Alan Wolfson.*

2. Most middle-level jobs should be conceived of as temporary.
3. Job incumbents are assigned to competence centers, which are also profit centers.
4. New dimensions for career development should be built into the system.

IDENTIFY AND FORM A SKELETON BUREAUCRACY

It is too much to expect that a business organization can completely eliminate the formal bureaucratic hierarchy. And there is little reason to think that it should. The major components of bureaucracy were invented for very logical reasons; those reasons still exist. Somebody has to run the show. Somebody has to provide direction, with some assurance that organization members will participate in moving toward that direction. There needs to be some rather clear definition of responsibility and authority for the organization to function rationally rather than randomly. There have to be certain guidelines or procedures and policies to guide the functioning of the organization.

But the problem is that bureaucracy has gotten too big and too pervasive. The new organization form of adhocracy would cut bureaucracy down to a mere skeleton. This would be done by identifying those key line management positions and functions where there is anticipated to be a clear continuing need for the position for at least, say, the next five to ten years. These key positions, such as certain department managers, the president and various vice-presidents, would form the skeleton bureaucracy of the adhocratic organization. But these positions, and perhaps a single assistant, would be the only permanent positions retained.

All staffs would be eliminated and a firm limit set on the size of the skeleton bureaucracy. Key executives would have policy-making responsibility for their functions and clearly defined but separate decision-making responsibility would be given to operating executives. When staff services were needed, members of the skeleton bureaucracy would "buy" them.

It is not difficult to think of taking a typical headquarters bureaucracy that might have, say, 900 people employed and reducing it to 45 or 50 persons. Traditional hierarchical arrangements of authority and responsibility would be maintained, and the allocation of resources to the skeleton bureaucracy would continue under traditional budgeting philosophies. However, because of the greatly reduced size of the skeleton bureaucracy, the visibility of activity, and the profitability criteria for its operations, the current games associated with the budgeting process should be significantly reduced.

ADHOCRATIC JOBS

All the jobs in the middle level of the organization would be adhocratic. This means that the position would be dissolved with the completion of an assignment. Organization members would be grouped by specialty areas according to their functional area of competence, the particular project they work on, or special areas of skill and expertise. These groupings would be formed into competence centers where organization members would function like consultants. All assignments to jobs from the competence centers would be of limited duration (perhaps limited to a maximum of two years or other appropriate duration). Assignments would be to various projects or task forces, similar to those in current matrix organizations. Or assignments would be made to staff projects serving the skeleton bureaucracy, both in the development of policy and in decision-making roles. But assignments would be temporary, and movement between centers and the skeleton bureaucracy would be fluid. There would be special provisions to insure the availability of information to members of the competence centers through comprehensive computer systems and full and open access to data.

PROFIT CENTERS

Competence centers would function as profit centers. This means that resources would be allocated to them on the basis of the demand for their services throughout the organization. Specific competence centers would compete with other centers and with outside consultants to obtain work. Most of their services would be for members of the skeleton bureaucracy on a fee basis. Rather than merely waiting for members of the skeleton bureaucracy to ask for their services, however, the members would be encouraged to go out seeking business. They would also be encouraged to develop project proposals for work by individuals or groups from the center and to develop joint ventures with outside consultants. Thus there would be a premium on looking for areas where individuals could make contributions—selling their services, developing proposals, and performing their functions in a competent and efficient (profitable) fashion. During slack periods, budgeting arrangements would permit continued attention to training and competence enhancement, as well as time for the development of proposals and profitable projects.

Compensation for employees of the competence centers would be based on some minimum rate plus a percentage commission based on their billable time as well as the quality of the performance they rendered to the customer. Quality and competence of services would be assessed periodically by evaluations from users within the skeleton bureaucracy. Compensation based on billable time would quickly clarify who was contributing to the needs of the organization. The evaluations, based purely on contributions to the profit objectives of the competence center, would eliminate the need for superior–subordinate-based appraisals. Various kinds of bonus plans could readily be built into the system. The compensation system would also include positive incentives and rewards for project proposals submitted to meet anticipated organizational needs. Additional compensation for the development of competencies in other members of the center would also be built into the system.

CAREER DEVELOPMENT

New forms of career development should be associated with membership in the competence center. First, assignments to a center would be temporary (perhaps two years' maximum), followed by a change of location and function to enhance personal growth. The concept includes more self-determination to enhance self-development through the premium placed on selling one's own ideas, developing proposals, looking for problems, and so forth. The key development item would be immediate feedback to the individual—whether his idea was accepted, whether somebody was willing to buy his services.

In place of a power-oriented hierarchy of titles and positions, titles in the competence center would be honorific. They would go with the man, not the position or kind of work—titles and levels would be based on competence, to be determined through peer nominations, much as in professional societies. An individual would be an assistant, then an associate, then a full specialist, with elections to "fellow" status. Guarantees of tenure and job security, just as in the university, would go along with increasing movement in the honorific and competence hierarchy.

Pensions and benefits would be portable. Rather than attempting to lock people into the organization through the design of pension plans, the company should assure them that they are free to leave if they want to. More flexibility to permit dual affiliations, part-time work, periodic sabbatical leaves, and the like would be built into career development in competence centers. Part of the compensation would have built into it an emphasis on the development of people relatively low in the honorific hierarchy through an on-the-job coaching and guidance procedure by people of "fellowship" or full "specialist" rank.

This is a basic framework of an adhocratic organization. Clearly, a great deal of further clarification needs to be done, and the various ramifications of such an approach have to be worked through. But there are a number of advantages in this basic framework.

1. First of all, it represents a fluid form of organization. It permits and encourages people to move to different projects and work assignments regularly. As such, it would help combat job decay, maintain job challenge, and maximize job development efforts.

2. The approach cuts down bureaucracy to a bare skeleton. Thus it removes much of the negative impact of hierarchy with its attendant dependency relationships, it increases the flow of information within the organization by simplifying it, and it clarifies the various interfaces in an organization so that organization development efforts can be focused most directly when and where they are needed. It saves all the positive aspects of bureaucracy and the rationality associated with it, yet cuts out most of the dysfunctional consequences. It also eliminates a lot of the superficial tasks and "fat" that find their way into most organizations and clearly identifies those people whom the skeleton bureaucracy is unwilling to fund or support.

3. The adhocratic system places a premium on competence. Presumably an authority system based on competence would be seen as more legitimate than the traditional hierarchical authority system. Pay, recognition, titles, and emphasis on development all would be based on competence. Incompetence would not last long in an adhocratic organization, and the inability to sell one's services is an objective indicator of incompetence.

4. Such an organization permits much better balancing of manpower. Competence centers can be kept lean,

with peak needs purchased on the outside if not available internally. It should minimize stockpiling of talent and overcome the problems of monopoly positions within organizations by having competence available in multiple centers. The utilization of skills should be much higher than in the traditional bureaucratic form.

The logical place for applying such a concept is in the middle levels, where bureaucracy resides in most organizations. But it's not too difficult to visualize its application to other functions, such as:

(a) *Computer services.* Competence centers could be set up from which a skeleton bureaucracy could buy programming, system support, and other data processing services, as they are often bought now from a service bureau.

(b) *Research and development.* It should be possible to buy, on a project basis, technical skills and project development teams who advance technology in particular areas.

(c) *Manufacturing.* Already many organizations subcontract a great deal of manufacturing. The adhocratic model would entail purchasing manufacturing internally, rather than necessarily subcontracting it to an outsider. Of course, subcontractors would be used as well. And manufacturing competence centers presumably would be free to sell their services to other organizations.

(d) *Marketing.* The concept could apply to such things as setting up franchises or buying marketing services on an adhocratic basis.

(e) *Rank and file employees.* Although it is difficult to think of the adhocratic competence center approach at the level of rank-and-file employees working in temporary groups, it is conceivable that the centers could be extended to that level, much as services are contracted for security guards, cafeterias, maintenance, or cleaning.

Clearly, there are many problems in the adhocratic model outlined here. We have presented just a bare framework. But this bare framework, when supplemented by the programs of individual development, job development, and organization development discussed earlier, could go a long way to resolving many of the problems besetting organizations today. Some such bold, imaginative new approach to organizations is needed. It will require considerable additional definition and refinement. But it will come. The time for this refinement and testing is now. The time when it may be too late is rapidly approaching. The motivation crisis in American industry demands that today's organizations move boldly into these new areas if they can hope to maintain their effectiveness through the 1970s and into the 1980s. The time for action is now.

REFERENCES

1. "Management Itself Holds the Key," *Business Week*, September 9, 1972.
2. A. K. Korman, *Industrial and Organizational Psychology* (Englewood Cliffs, N.J.: Prentice Hall, 1971).
3. J. W. Forrester, "A New Corporate Design," *Industrial Management Review*, Fall 1965, pp. 5–17.
4. R. E. Walton, "How to Counter Alienation in the Plant," *Harvard Business Review*, November–December 1972, pp. 70–81.

INDEX